HISTORIC NORTH COUNTRY

DISASTERS

CHERI L. FARNSWORTH

THE
History
PRESS

Published by The History Press
Charleston, SC
www.historypress.com

Copyright © 2020 by Cheri L. Farnsworth
All rights reserved

First published 2020

Manufactured in the United States

ISBN 9781467145008

Library of Congress Control Number: 2019951840

I dedicate this book to my first grandchild, Benjamin—my heart and my inspiration. You light up this world with an energy that extends far beyond your pint-sized frame. Leaving blessings and joy in your wake, you are the ultimate antithesis to the disaster and despair I speak of here. Shine on, sweet boy.

CONTENTS

CONTENTS

PREFACE

While every effort was made to obtain original photographs or sketches of each locale or disaster described in this book, in some cases, it was necessary to improvise and use images of similar events from the period that best depict what I believe the details of the stories I wrote to be. The credit line will indicate from whom or which source the image was obtained. Where original photographs and photo postcards I've collected over the years were used, the credit line says simply *Author's collection.*

ACKNOWLEDGEMENTS

I'd like to thank my acquisitions editor, J. Banks Smither, for his enthusiasm and expertise. And many thanks to Abigail Fleming, my copyeditor, for keeping me on track and making me look good. Appreciation also goes to Crystal Murray, senior sales specialist, and Cameron Haines, who designed the impressive cover.

I always know I'm in good hands with The History Press and Arcadia Publishing.

Many thanks to Tom LaClair, Clayton historian, who was especially helpful with my "Christmas Eve Munitions Plant Explosion" story, since two of his great-uncles were among the unfortunate victims. The suggestions and assistance of Carol Haber, researcher, Adirondack History Center Museum; Sharron Hewston, town of Jay historian; and Clifton town historian Mark Friden were all very useful. Much appreciation goes, as well, to Kimberly Hayden, records management specialist/historian at the Jefferson County Clerk's Office, for her kind offer of assistance; and to JeanMarie Martello, archivist at the St. Lawrence County Historical Association, for her willingness to help me track down local disasters. MaryEllen Casselman of the Massena Museum (the Celine G. Philibert Memorial Culture Centre & Museum) was so generous in locating and providing images, as were Ellen O'dair of the Brockville Museum; Don Smith of the Stormont, Dundas and Glengarry Historical Society; and John Gleed of St. Lawrence Piks. I appreciate you all so much.

Much of the research for this book came from old newspaper articles digitized by the NYS Historic Newspapers project online. What an incredible resource to have at our fingertips! I am so grateful for their efforts to preserve our history in this way. For researchers and historians, it's truly a treasure-trove.

It goes without saying that the support and enthusiasm of our loved ones sustains us all. In my case, a simple "thank-you" hardly seems adequate, considering what my family has seen me through the past couple years, but I extend a full-hearted thank-you, nevertheless, to my husband, Leland, and my four beautiful daughters: Michelle Revai; Jamie (and Benny and Dan) Beaudoin; Katie Revai and her fiancé, Kyle LeFevre; and Nicole Revai. You guys are my heroes and my blessings. Thank you for keeping me tethered and grounded when I find myself drifting a bit too far "out there." Please don't ever be afraid to reel me back in—in fact, I'm counting on you for it.

With undying gratitude, I lovingly acknowledge my late father, Thomas Raymond Dishaw. Dad used to tell me about some of the disasters I've included here. I think he would have liked this book. Also counted among my dearest blessings is my beautiful mother, Jean; my brother, Tom Dishaw; and my sisters, Cindy Barry and Chris Hargadin, along with their wonderful, expanding families. Life goes on, against all odds, we've learned. Haven't we?

I thank God and my lucky stars for this precious family of mine—each and every one of them. Too often, I immerse myself in the past doing research for regional history books, but family has a way of instantly snapping me back to the present and promising an absolutely, positively, supercalifragilisticexpialidocious tomorrow. Right, Benny?

INTRODUCTION

There were many times, while penning this book of doom and destruction, that I spoke of fate and destiny or of Lady Luck looking favorably—or unfavorably—on someone. *His fate was then sealed....Lady Luck cast her fair hand....It was a situation destined to repeat itself...* As it turns out, I was on to something there without even realizing it until just now as I scribble down my intro (last, as always). An obsolete definition of disaster is an "unfavorable aspect of a planet or star." Indeed, the old Italian word *disastro* comes from the Latin *dis*, meaning a "negative effect," and *astro*, "star." If that definition of disaster is taken at its word—then disasters (and the role we play in them) are already predetermined. In other words, unless it's *not* our appointed time to die, we will die at a specific and inescapable time (whether by accident, illness, old age, disaster or countless other scenarios).

Whether you subscribe to such pseudoscience or not, the fact is that when we have a "date" with disaster, we may find ourselves among those being saved by heroes, or we may play the role of hero; we may be among those who stand by helplessly, forced to bear witness; or we may be among those who never stood a chance of surviving. We may feel somehow prompted to step outside for a smoke just seconds before the old tinderbox we call home goes up in flames, or we may be the poor soul who hesitates for too long at the third-floor window with its curtains in flames. We may happen to be on leave the day the freighter that employs us explodes, or we may happen to be on our very first day of work on that same doomed freighter when it tragically goes down in flames. When disaster strikes, we may live, or we may die; we may bear witness; we may save the day; or we may simply hear about it and shake our heads sympathetically. But eventually, our time, too, will come—whether gently in our sleep or not so gently as we play or work. Henry Wadsworth Longfellow famously said, "Thy fate is the common fate of all; into each life, some rain must fall." You will see those words in action repeatedly throughout this book. Ultimately, we all share a common fate (death). All that differs is *how*, *where* and *when* we will face it.

The following stories of disaster depict a wide range of tragic events that befell our ancestors. Most of them will not be personally recalled by those younger than seventy-five or eighty years of age—since they took place between 1845 and 1947—but the children and grandchildren of those involved may remember hearing the tragic stories retold in hushed tones at family gatherings. I found the sheer volume of calamities our forefathers faced to be astounding, and I touched on only a handful of them. As in my previous works, I lean toward resurrecting stories that have long been forgotten by many so that new and future generations of North Country residents will learn of our past tragedies and triumphs and know of the tough stock we northern New Yorkers come from. Our predecessors had a great sense of community, faith and determination that carried them through the unthinkable dangers so prevalent during their lifetimes. Their legacy has been left in all that we see around us today. We've inherited their estates, their farms, their factories, their camps and their towns and cities. And I believe we also inherited their strength and determination and that it will hold us in good stead, should we ever experience the unimaginable as they did.

Thankfully, many of yesteryears' common disasters are rarely heard of today (industrial and hotel fires, train wrecks, shipwrecks and mine or factory explosions). You never see entire towns wiped out by fire anymore—at least not around here—and you certainly don't see children working in dangerous factories or engaged in target practice around explosives. Tremendous strides in hazard prevention and safety precautions have been made in the past hundred years on local, state and federal levels. Whereas man-made disasters once seemed to outnumber natural disasters, today it's the other way around. Natural disasters (ice storms, earthquakes, flooding, forest fires, blizzards, high winds and so on) will always exist, but we don't have the control over them that we now have in preventing the careless, man-made disasters so prevalent in our past. Natural disasters cannot be regulated and are difficult, if not impossible, to contain. We can, however, arm ourselves with knowledge, familiarize ourselves with contingency plans, maintain adequate survival supplies and learn from past mistakes. Learn from our ancestors so that their struggles and terrible losses were not in vain. General George S. Patton said, "Prepare for the unknown by studying how others in the past have coped with the unforeseeable and the unpredictable." We should remain ever-vigilant and be prepared—on both a personal and a public level—to handle potential disaster scenarios that could arise. Simply put, we should keep calm…but "prep" on.

1

EF5 TORNADO

PHILADELPHIA AND NORTHERN NEW YORK, 1845–1995

Northern New York is no stranger to devastating incidents involving wind. Strong winds have been the driving force behind our blizzards and nor'easters, our lake effect snows and our Great Lakes gales and squalls. And let's not forget wind's reckless complicity in the most destructive fires our region has experienced. But this story is primarily about tornadoes, wind shears and microbursts—atmospheric events in which wind, and wind alone, causes massive destruction and sometimes death.

On July 15, 1995, an unforgettable microburst killed five people, injured eleven and damaged almost 1 million acres of land, leveling over 100,000 acres of timber in the Adirondack Park alone. The derecho, as it was officially termed, reached wind speeds of up to 100 miles per hour on its deadly trek through Upstate New York. Prior to that was the "Big Blowdown" of 1950 with wind speeds that climbed to 100 miles per hour—certainly powerful enough to destroy or damage over 800,000 acres in the Adirondacks and leave thousands without power for two weeks. Only a handful of Jefferson County octogenarians and nonagenarians will personally recall the more isolated Philadelphia tornado of 1935 that leveled the Earl Drake farm and home, tragically killing his wife and daughter and injuring two others. Continuing back on the timeline, there was a mighty tornado in July 1856 that swept through Franklin County, claiming the life of one unfortunate soul. In the towns of Constable, Burke and Chateaugay, hundreds of buildings were moved from their foundations, unroofed or utterly destroyed. The *New York Times* of July 9, 1856, said the "fearful tornado"

Rural tornado damage. *Author's collection.*

did an "incalculable amount of damage, sweeping down forests, scattering fences, destroying all manner of buildings and other property, and leaving nothing but desolation in its track."

There was one wind event, however, that set the bar for all others that would follow. They called it the "Great Windfall." On September 20, 1845, an ominous tornado formed over Lake Ontario and tore through parts of Jefferson, St. Lawrence, Franklin and Essex Counties before finally crossing Lake Champlain and entering Vermont in a much-weakened state. Clifton town historian Mark Friden told me that meteorologists of today would likely have considered it a rare EF5—the most powerful tornado known to man on the widely used Enhanced Fujita scale—with wind speeds over two hundred miles per hour and the capability of producing "incredible damage." The fact that the local population was sparse in the mid-1800s was a blessing for sure. There would have been a much greater loss of life had the tornado happened when the area became more populated years later. Yet it is also because of the paucity of population that firsthand accounts of the event were scarce, as were the number of local news sources operating in the area at that time. The *Essex County Republican* of September 27, 1845, said:

> *So far as we have learned, the ravages of the storm commenced at Union Falls, making a complete wreck of many of the buildings in that place, and for a distance…trees, fences, barns and houses were leveled with the ground.…The brick school house near the Travis forge in Peru was utterly demolished, and the brick dwelling of H.N. Peabody nearby was partially destroyed. We hear of two houses that were blown down over the heads of the inmates, and it is most extraordinary that no lives were lost.…*
>
> *Mr. Rogers of Forksville was crossing the Little Ausable north of Peru village when the blow reached him, giving himself, horse and carriage a complete somersault into the river, scattering the plank of the bridge in every direction. By a remarkable providence no injury was done to Mr. Rogers or his team, beyond the unpleasant circumstances of a dunking in the mud of the creek.*

In St. Lawrence County, ten thousand acres were left in ruin in the towns of Fowler and Edwards alone. The *Watertown Jeffersonian* of September 20, 1845, reported, "In all this distance there is not a building, nor a tree of any description left standing—all were prostrated by its mighty force—leaving widespread ruin and desolation as evidence of its fearful power." Strangely enough, even though sixteen structures were swept away in the destruction, nobody was killed or even seriously injured in those towns. From Antwerp in Jefferson County, the tornado appeared to have traveled at about fifty miles per hour through St. Lawrence County. The *Jeffersonian* offered the following harrowing experiences endured that day:

> *Crossing the Oswegatchie, the next settlement in the line of the tempest was on the Pitcairn road, embracing ten buildings.…Mr. Brown had recently erected a 40 by 30 barn which he had filled with the products of his farm. This, with his house, was blown down and the contents scattered far and wide. Mr. Brown was taken up and carried 15 to 20 rods* [around one hundred yards]*, unconscious of the moving power, and was severely bruised upon his head, shoulders and other parts of his body. When he struck the ground, he seized hold of a stump and by that means saved himself from further personal injury.*

Left: *Child at a Writing Desk* by Alexandre Antigna, circa 1887. *Wikimedia Commons*.

Below: Freak northeast gale topples trees. *NOAA's National Weather Service (NWS) Collection*.

Incredibly, a wood-frame schoolhouse next to Brown's property was moved entirely off its foundation, yet the teacher and students within remained unscathed.

The next house south of Mr. Brown was that of Mr. Leonard in which there were two women and five children. Hearing the noise of the tornado and seeing its approach, these also took refuge in the cellar. One of the women last descending was struck by the timbers of the house as it moved and rendered senseless, in which condition she remained nearly a day.

Next to Mr. Leonard's stood another house—the name of the occupant not given—in which was a sick woman and a young child about three weeks old and a young woman named Kinney who was attending upon her. Frightened by the noise and the looks of the tempest as it approached, Miss Kinney threw herself upon another bed in the same room when the house was blown down, and one of the logs of which it was composed fell across the bed and Miss Kinney and held her fast. The sick woman immediately rose from her bed and by almost superhuman strength removed the log and thus saved the life of the young woman.

Near this latter house, in the street, was a man driving a yoke of oxen attached to a wagon laden with coal.... Two large trees were brought by the wind and laid across the wagon, crushing it without injury to the team or to the man, except the tearing of his clothes and slight scratches on his person. The team was so bound in by the trees and rubbish that it required several hours to extricate them, which was not effective until the Monday following.

The village of Malone in Franklin County also had its stories to tell. Many of the homes and barns there lost their roofs or were destroyed. In one fallen house, three small children were buried under debris, yet they miraculously survived unscathed. The windfall continued its path of destruction, reaching "a new village and extensive iron works near Keeseville, Essex County, which it entirely destroyed." When the tornado finally died out, as they eventually do, a storm of tremendous hail followed, maiming cattle, pets and other critters exposed to the elements. The sheer size, strength, speed and scale of this tornado had never been seen before, nor since, in Northern New York. For this reason, historian Friden called it the "granddaddy of them all."

WATERTOWN IN RUINS

WATERTOWN, 1849

As weary travelers and long-term tenants slumbered obliviously at the American Hotel on Court Street early one spring morning in 1849, a monster with a ravenous appetite had sprung into action below, intent on devouring everything in its path, save stone or mortar. In a frenzied state of insatiable hunger and impossible speed, it taunted its would-be dousers—the early Watertown volunteer firefighters summoned to defeat it—as if to say catch me, if you can. One can imagine the plight of the people, as they awakened one by one to the growing chorus of screams. *Fire! Fire!* The fire chief would have been evaluating the situation on horse and shouting orders through a speaking trumpet, but he could barely have been heard over the roar of the fire and panic in the streets. Many fled their homes, hotels and tenements in their nightclothes—the men and boys in nightshirts and caps, à la Scrooge in *A Christmas Carol*, the women and girls in modest, high-collared, white cotton nightgowns and sleep bonnets or kerchiefs. If time permitted, others would surely have attempted to change into their daytime clothing before joining those already in the streets. Regardless of what they were wearing, all undoubtedly shared the same horror as they watched the scene unfolding before them.

According to *Watertown Daily Times* reporter Chris Brock in his 2017 article about the fire department's 200th anniversary, the Watertown Fire Department was created in 1817, at a time when every house in town was mandated to have two large buckets available at all times for each floor of the structure, in case fire erupted anywhere within the vicinity. When needed,

Early view of Watertown, late 1800s. *Author's collection.*

these buckets would be passed out of every home and filled with water for those fighting the fires, which included all males over fourteen years of age. Men and boys, young and old, were required to head directly to all structure fires on horse or foot, or they could face ten days in jail, not to mention the shame of cowardice.

In 1849, when the American Hotel fire began, a village water system was still a few years in the offing, so the primary source of water for firefighting was limited to natural spring water from the village's public square. The tenacity and grit of the bucket brigade, while admirable and efficient under normal circumstances (such as a single-structure fire), was no match for the largest fire in Watertown's early history. According to the *Jeffersonian, Extra* of May 13, 1849, the 3:00 a.m. fire was believed to have started in either a rear building of the hotel or at the back of L. Paddock's adjoining store. The article, titled "Great Conflagration," said:

> *At first the supposition prevailed that the fire was the work of an incendiary* [device]*; but we are happy to state, for the credit of our village and human nature, that it probably arose from the spontaneous combustion of some kind of chemicals stored by Mr. Druggist Camp, in Paddock's back store.*

Unidentified view of Boston fire aftermath, 1872, by Holton and Robinson. *Wikimedia Commons.*

A further explanation was added as a postscript at the end of that article:

It is thought the fire originated in the Woodhouse of the American, from several leaches which had the day before been set up. Old barrels with Stone Lime at the bottom and ashes rammed in on top. This might ignite, and probably did.

Whatever the origin, the ignition quickly morphed from spark to flicker, then flicker to flame in the usual manner. The resultant explosion, coupled with a fair breeze blowing from the southeast, carried the fire swiftly from there, engulfing over one hundred buildings, homes and businesses in the vicinities of Arsenal and Court Streets. Virtually the entire business section of Watertown had fallen. Besides the American Hotel and its outbuildings, the fire destroyed Paddock's Block and all of its stores, Fairbank's Block, C. Calhoun's blocks and Woodruff's new Iron Block. It toppled the Trinity Church and its steeple with the town clock and engulfed at least thirty stores, the Episcopal church, the Columbia Hotel, three printing offices—including the *Northern State Journal* and *Democratic Union*—three banks and the post office.

It seemed as if nothing could stop it and that no building would be spared. But when the blaze reached the Jefferson County Clerk's Office, which was made of stone, the beast finally met an unwavering opponent. The fireproof structure had but one weak spot—a wooden roof—and that was purposely lifted off just in time, leaving nothing more to fuel the flames north along Court Street. The same gentle wind that carried the flames north toward the stone structure prevented the flames from any southward progression. As dawn broke a few hours later, the weary, shaken residents beheld the full scope of devastation to their homes and livelihoods and a much-needed rain began to fall, snuffing out the last of the embers. "The destruction is appalling," according to the *Jeffersonian, Extra*, "far exceeding anything Jefferson County has experienced before." An unfortunate woman and several horses were discovered in the ashes, the *Jeffersonian, Extra* reported:

> *The remains of a human body were found where some stage carriages were burned, supposed to be those of a frail sister who had been refused admission during the evening, where she had called for lodging. Some six or eight horses were burned* [as well].

The Poor Woman by Alexandre Antigna, circa 1887. *Wikimedia Commons.*

Aside from the tragic loss of life on which a price cannot be placed, loss of property was estimated to be around $250,000 (over $8 million in today's dollars). Insurance ultimately covered approximately half of that total. Many of the businesses were covered in full, with many others covered perhaps for three-quarters of their losses. But the greatest loss, according to the *Jeffersonian*, was felt not by the wealthy businessmen and the well-known movers and shakers of Watertown society but rather by those of the lower classes who were unable to afford any fire insurance at all. The paper said:

> *In the main, the losses have fallen on men able to bear them. But for this fact, the gloom would be greatly increased. But while those remarks hold good to a great extent, truth compels us to show the dark side of the picture. Several owners and occupants of tenements—families in indigent circumstances, clerks, artisans, boarders, etc. have lost their all. On such, the loss falls heavily—severely—and appeals most eloquently to the sympathies of our fellow citizens in other towns and counties. A Relief Committee will cheerfully receive and apply such donations as money, goods and clothing as their benevolence may confide to their care.*

As bleak as the situation appeared at the time, the fire became the catalyst for a glorious rebirth and success story of our North Country ancestors. Like the mighty phoenix of myth, Watertown rose from its ashes better, larger and stronger than ever before—thanks to the tireless efforts of those resourceful, hardworking, determined men and women of nineteenth-century Jefferson County who rolled up their sleeves and set about vigorously rebuilding their city.

3

WHITNEY MARBLE COMPANY BOILER EXPLOSION

GOUVERNEUR, 1884

The Whitney Marble Company, about three-quarters of a mile outside of Gouverneur, experienced a devastating explosion on Saturday morning, May 3, 1884, that leveled the sawmill and claimed six lives. "Five men were hurled instantly into eternity, and two others [were believed to be] fatally injured," according to an article in the *Ogdensburg Daily Journal* on May 5, 1884. Two days later, the *Gouverneur Free Press* chimed in and described it as "by far the greatest calamity that ever befell our village." The *Free Press* reporter was one of the first on the scene and "was astonished to find the works entirely demolished, the debris covering the ground for a distance of several hundred feet, while the bodies of five of the unfortunate workmen lay mangled, crushed, and scalded among and around the ruins. It was a sight to make the stoutest heart quail."

The marble company had been formed just two years earlier by a group of New York City and local investors and entrepreneurs. In October 1883, it began preparing the renowned Gouverneur marble for market. The machinery for the marble works was driven by an eighty-horsepower engine housed in a sixty-by-eighty-foot wooden structure called the sawmill. The sawmill, where the explosion occurred, contained the engine, the powerful boilers and four "gang saws" used to cut blocks of marble into slabs. The cause of the explosion was initially undetermined, but two boilers that had been inspected and deemed dangerous by a local mechanic had just been repaired by Joseph Olive and Oliver Dashneau that fateful morning. The Watertown Steam Engine Company, from which the boilers were

Marble quarry workers and management in Gouverneur, circa 1895–1900. *From the collections of the St. Lawrence County Historical Association.*

purchased the previous year, sent the two men by train from Watertown to Gouverneur to repair the equipment. They expected to return home that evening. Instead, they were apparently at ground zero of the disaster, for they were last seen on top of one of the boilers, attempting to bring it to full steam for the first time since its repair just moments before the blast. To give you an idea of just how powerful an explosion it was, the half-ton dome of that iron boiler was thrown more than one hundred feet by the blast, and witnesses said the roof of the building lifted into the air, with debris flying in every direction. We can only imagine what such force would do to a mere mortal.

In those days, one did not have to imagine, because newspaper accounts described such horrific scenes in graphic detail. Today, a more tactful approach is taken when reporting scenes of death, out of respect for victims' families; but reporters of the late nineteenth century were under no such constraints in their reporting protocol. Family members, along with every other person reading the newspapers, learned precisely how the victims of disaster had died and how their bodies were discovered. For example, the *New York Times* of May 4, 1884, reported:

The trunk of Dashneau's body was discovered hanging over a beam in the debris. His arms and limbs were scattered about the building, but his head has not yet been found. Olive's head was torn off at the upper jaw. Both bodies were entirely stripped of clothing.

The *Gouverneur Free Press* listed the dead:

Joseph Olive and Oliver Dashneau were boiler makers from Watertown N.Y. and in the employ of the Watertown Steam Engine Co., and were sent here to repair the boilers at the "Marble Works." Oliver leaves a wife and six children, dependent on him for support. Dashneau leaves a wife and one child.

Walter Frank Newcombe was the engineer in charge and was from Depeyster, N.Y. He was 35 years of age, a widower, and leaves one child....Eli Jackson, workman, resided in this town, was a married man and leaves a widow and three children. He was 33 years of age....W.T. Miller was a citizen of this town and about 48 years of age....he leaves a wife and four children....Charles Murray who was fatally injured died

Gouverneur marble quarry pit, circa 1890–1900. *From the collections of the St. Lawrence County Historical Association.*

at 5:30 o'clock p.m. Saturday, the day of the explosion. He has been a resident here for nearly three years, was unmarried and 20 years of age.... It is said he was soon to be married to a highly-respected lady of this place.

Morris O'Harran, a workman, was blown out of the building a distance of 25 to 40 feet into the meadow towards the road. He was badly bruised about the body, and his head cut severely. It is thought he will recover.

The full-page article added:

The soles of Jackson's boots were blown off while they were on his feet and were found inside the building, the boot legs still adhering to his body. The heads of Dashneau and Oliver were blown clean off, and one of their bodies was found hanging across a beam, having neither head nor limbs.

The *Times*, in theorizing the cause of the blast, noted:

The cause of the explosion is unknown, but it is supposed that one of the workmen [Dashneau or Olive] *opened a valve leading from the boiler with a full head of steam* [90 pounds] *to the boiler having but 15 pounds of steam on, and the expansion on top was so much greater than that at the bottom, which contained water, that the boiler was forced to give way. A coroner's jury was at once impaneled and an investigation was begun.... The damage to the works is estimated at $25,000. The building will probably be rebuilt at once.*

A coroner's inquest commenced within hours of the accident, and the employer, foreman, witnesses and experts were questioned at length and in painstaking detail. George Marshall had been foreman of the company's boiler shop in Syracuse for twenty years. Within a week, on May 8, 1884, the jury had reached its verdict. According to the *Watertown Daily Times* of May 8, 1884:

The coroner's inquest concluded its labors rather unexpectedly about 12 o'clock today. The verdict of the jury was that Oliver Dashneau, Joseph Olive, Eli Jackson, W.T. Miller, Charles Murray, and W.F. Newcomb came to their deaths by an explosion of the boiler in the Whitney Marble Company's works Saturday last. The explosion was caused neither by defective workmanship, nor imperfect material, nor lack of water, but by excessive pressure, probably produced by the openings of the connection of

Teacher with her students in front of Star Lake School, circa 1910. *From the collections of the St. Lawrence County Historical Association.*

the two boilers by some person unknown, there being 90 to 95 pounds of pressure in one boiler, and 80 to 85 pounds pressure in the other, the low pressure boiler exploding.

When all was said and done, fifteen children did not see their fathers come home that horrific day—a scenario all too common in the days before workplace safety regulations. In 1884, the families of workers killed on the job were probably compensated about half the time, if that, and not very generously. Before regulations held employers responsible for a safe work environment, employers had little incentive to invest in safer practices, because if sued, they could argue that the employee had assumed the risk when he took the job or that it was the employee's fault and not the fault of the employer. When industrial accidents occurred, coroner's inquests were often hastily arranged, employers were typically found not at fault (as in the case of the Whitney Marble Company boiler explosion) and the show, as they say, would go on. Before the dust had even settled at the site of this disaster—indeed, before all the victims had even been buried—the company boasted that it would be up and running again quickly.

4

CARTHAGE IN RUINS

CARTHAGE AND WEST CARTHAGE, 1884

They called it "the most terrible fire in the history of Northern New York." The great Carthage fire destroyed nearly $8 million (today's value) worth of property, which included all of the manufactories, some two hundred dwellings, four churches, hotels, schools and an opera house. It left multiple streets in ruins and hundreds of people homeless. But within every crisis is an opportunity to shine. And shine the North Country did. The tireless relief efforts and selfless acts of kindness from neighboring communities in the days following the Carthage disaster proved that brotherly love was alive and well in Northern New York, even in its earliest days and most trying tribulations. As one early *Watertown Times* reporter noted poetically, "The results of yesterday in this city prove that one touch of sorrow makes the whole world kin." You will understand why in a moment. First, let's set the scene of the disaster.

A strong wind was blowing in from the southwest, making the cool fall morning seem all the chillier. With an average temperature for that date of forty-five degrees Fahrenheit and a strong wind of, say, thirty miles per hour, the temperature felt like just thirty-six degrees that day. The trees in every yard and park had mostly lost their foliage, leaving the branches and trunks naked and exposed to the increasing cold. It seems a backward thing, doesn't it? That trees should lose their leaves before winter, just when one would think they would need the added insulation the most? But all it takes is a steady wind conspiring with a heavy rain to leave a tree with thousands of red and orange leaves barren in a single day's time. In this region,

State Street, Carthage, circa 1902. *Author's collection.*

wind conspires with cold for some brutal, downright life-threatening wind chills, so we bundle up. It conspires with snow to create the blizzards and nor'easters that every schoolchild prays for and every adult dreads, so we dig ourselves out. We're a hardy lot. We know how to deal with those things, for the most part. But then there's wind conspiring with fire. Now that's a whole different animal. It is the most dreaded wind combination of all, for it can be unpredictable, fast-moving and merciless, completely devastating a large area in a very short amount of time. In Carthage, on October 20, 1884, this was a recipe for disaster.

Around eleven o'clock on that ill-fated Monday morning, a fire broke out in the P.L. & C.E. Eaton sash and blind factory in West Carthage. It is believed to have been caused by sparks from the smokestack of Revell's tannery. The alarm was sounded at 11:10 a.m., and church bells rang as the fire greedily ravaged one factory or mill after another on the west side of the Black River, prompting the fire department volunteers—armed with their steamer and hose cars—on the east side to race across the bridge. Besides Eaton's factory, it destroyed Harvey Farrar's tub factory and the Mayer, Ross & Company's furniture factory and consumed 125 cords of hemlock from Revell's tannery. Dead leaves ignited and were carried ablaze by the wind across the water to Guyot's and then Furnace Islands as the fire worked 's way toward the mainland and the heart of the village. According to the *Lewis County Democrat* of October 22, 1884:

> *Sparks flew across Black river, a distance of nearly a half mile, while the Carthage fire department was engaged on the west side, and ignited all the property upon Guyot's island devoted to manufacturing. Guyot's planing mill, Pratt's shingle mill, and other property. From the planing mill, the fire spread to Spring street, and from thence to Mechanic street and Church street. Fires by this time were raging in half a dozen directions, and any attempt to save the village from destruction seemed fruitless. A stiff breeze spread the flames so rapidly that half a dozen new dwellings would be enveloped while the stream from an engine was directed upon one.*

Around noon, the Lowville volunteer fire department received a dispatch requesting the men's assistance in Carthage. They immediately assembled and secured a special train to take the firefighters, their steamer, the LaFrance and their hose cart to their sister village, arriving in just twenty-two minutes. Likewise, the Watertown department was called when it became apparent that the manpower on hand was not enough to bring the fire under control due to changes in wind direction, and it arrived with its steamer just moments before the Lowville crew. The *Watertown Re-Union* of October 22, 1884, said:

> *When Chief Cole arrived at 1 p.m. he found that the fire had crossed the railroad track, in several different places. He at once took charge and worked ahead of the fire. The Watertown department pumped both reservoirs dry in half an hour and then the Carthage steamer had to be put to work filling them. With water enough, much property could have been saved. The fire burned itself out in many places, or it could not have been controlled. Streets, yards, and porches are full of household goods.*

The LaFrance steamer was moved to the bank of the Black River at the foot of Spring Street, where it was able to "throw three streams incessantly through sixteen hundred feet of hose," for what it was worth at that point, according to the *Democrat*. Even with the full force of the Carthage, Watertown and Lowville fire departments battling the blaze, the conflagration continued to elude their full grasp and any attempts to bring it under control. The *Democrat* stated:

At three o'clock it seemed as if no power on earth could stay the destruction of the whole village. House after house was swept away, and the heat and smoke was so intense that it was impossible to go from one portion of the village to another. Both sides of State street were in flames, and the whole northern extremity of the village was a sheet of fire, the conflagration extending at the upper end of the village across State street to West street.

The burned district embraces the finest resident[ial] portions of the village, and upwards of two hundred manufactories, churches, schools, residences and barns were burned. Of residences alone, there were more than one hundred destroyed.

The *Watertown Re-Union* of October 22, 1884, reported:

It looked as if the entire business portion of the village would be burned. Chief William H. Cole of Watertown kindly took command of the various departments. He put his steamer on State street, which is the main street of the village, placing the Carthage steamer at the river and getting his stream from it. The Lowville steamer was placed at Ryther & Pringle's pound. Thus, there was a steamer on each side of the fire, one east and the other west of the main street, fighting at the very center of the fire. The firemen were able to get it under control by five o'clock on West street. This proved [to be] the salvation of the business portion of the village.

More than one hundred families, both wealthy and poor, were displaced from their wooden homes that had burned down. Not even half of those homes were insured, and the rest were not insured enough. Families were sleeping in their barns, if the barns were still standing, and in the fields, fully exposed to the elements, trying to protect what few belongings, if any, they had time to grab before fleeing their homes. At least twelve streets were involved: Spring, Furnace, Washington, Mechanic, School, Church, Budd, Fulton, State, Clinton, West and James. In all, some two hundred structures, including the homes, had been destroyed. The Baptist, Episcopal, Presbyterian and Disciple churches were all destroyed, along with the engine house, many factories, the town hall, the schools, the opera house and Peck's hotel. After the fire finally spent itself and was brought under control around 5:00 p.m., seventy acres of populated land was left smoldering.

Although it had robbed Carthage of so much materially, the fire had not claimed a single life. "Several people were injured by falling debris, or from prostration," according to the *Democrat*, and a dozen firemen suffered minor injuries. But no lives were lost, and that was a miracle. Now began the difficult task of cleaning up, taking stock of needs and rebuilding. The residents of Carthage and nearby towns really stepped up to the plate. The *Lewis County Democrat* described the earliest relief efforts in its October 22, 1884 edition:

> *About four o'clock, the hook and ladder truck from Lowville arrived on the regular train, and it did able assistance in pulling down buildings. At about five o'clock, the spread of the fire had seemingly spent itself, and at 6:45, the steamer from Boonville arrived. Utica's fire department, not appreciating the magnitude of the fire, or for some other reason, failed to arrive. About eight o'clock, the Lowville fire department with its apparatus returned to Lowville upon a special train provided by General Manager Maynard. The Boonville steamer took their place and played upon the ruins through the night to prevent further spread.*
>
> *The people of Carthage bear their sufferings heroically, and those who were fortunate enough to escape thankfully lend what aid they can in assisting the hundred other families who were rendered homeless. General Manager Maynard telegraphed his conductors to pass all the fire sufferers to any position [along] the road where they had friends....During the fire, families were separated, and the frantic terror displayed by some was terrible to witness. Others were apparently calm and collected and did much valuable service in their own behalf and in assisting others.*

The *Watertown Re-Union* commented, "The people of the village were very kind to firemen and to the fire sufferers, but the town, never very rich, is now poorer than ever. But one store is burned, that of Mr. Mills. Many of the people burned out will have to leave here, as there are no houses to shelter and no work to support them." A great deal of people had been employed at the many factories and mills that burned down, leaving them without jobs to support their families. It would not be an easy climb back to what had been, but there was certainly no shortage of helping hands from nearby communities. Watertown, which had suffered its own devastating fire thirty-five years earlier, offered large donations of cash and clothing. The *Watertown Times* of October 24, 1884, said:

> *Besides the liberal donations of cash, the amount of clothing sent in to the committee was simply wonderful. Last night six large packing cases full of*

men's, women's and children's wearing apparel stood ready for shipment in the hallway of Washington hall, while the floor of the Y.M.C.A. lecture room was more than three-quarters covered with piles of clothing of all descriptions and sizes. In fact, Secretary Speares said, there was enough there to clothe all of Carthage. This is very encouraging and proves that the people of Watertown are wide awake to the needs of their brethren and will do their share, and more, to alleviate the suffering which the coming long and cold winter must necessarily entail upon them.

Besides clothing, residents of the city of Watertown donated a total of $4,250.25 by the time the paper went to print, the equivalent of a staggering $110,000 in today's dollars—not a bad haul for four days' time. There were many stories of random acts of kindness by individuals as well, like this note in the *Times*: "Clint Rider's patrons received no ice yesterday, for the reason that he devoted the day to gathering clothing for the sufferers while he was busy with a subscription paper. Clint has a heart as big as an ox."

Utica, too, stepped up to the plate. The mayor called a meeting at city hall to discuss taking action that would substantially help those in need in Carthage. Multiple committees were established to secure donations and funding toward that effort. The *Times* said:

There is an urgent need of prompt action. One dollar now is as good as two will be by and by. The people have present wants which demand attention. It is expected that the various ward committees will go to work and canvas their respective sections at once. Daily deposits should be made with Mr. John Goodale at the First national bank. The ladies of the Women's Christian Union will attend to packing and shipping all contributions of clothes or household goods of any sort that may be left at the Industrial home on Court street. Utica should not let any other city outdo her in generosity.

Even New York City began a movement to assist Carthage. The *Watertown Times* of October 25, 1884, noted:

A movement to raise funds and clothing for the sufferers by the great fire at Carthage is now in progress in this city, and promises to result in the collection of a large sum of money and other necessities of life. This charitable step was taken by several businessmen of this city, whose early home was in Carthage or its vicinity. They are circulating subscription papers among the wealthy merchants of the metropolis, and urging them to contribute either money, clothing or anything else to relieve the distress of the burned-out families.

By October 25, just five days after the fire, the *Times* reported that $10,000 had been raised by various towns and cities—more than $250,000 by today's standards. So many clothes were donated that Carthage had to request a hold on any more incoming shipments of clothing. Instead, residents requested boots, shoes, rubbers and stoves. The funds raised surely went far in allowing that request to be fulfilled. It is truly a testament to the generosity of North Country citizens toward those in need that a devastated community found itself with a supply of donated items greater than the need.

5

BLOWN TO ATOMS

PLATTSBURGH, 1887

Even in the late 1800s, word traveled fairly fast and surprisingly far, especially when disaster struck anywhere in the continental United States, thanks to the electric telegraph and travel by rail. The *New York Times*, being a daily and much larger newspaper than those of rural Northern New York, often carried briefs about local calamities before the small towns in which the calamities occurred had even published their own accounts. This was the case on February 25, 1886, when the *Times* ran a brief initial summary about an explosion in Plattsburgh that had occurred the day before:

> *A DYNAMITE EXPLOSION. Plattsburgh, N.Y., Feb. 24—An explosion of dynamite occurred this afternoon at the works of the Clinton Powder Company, two miles from this village. One building was demolished. William P. Foss, Superintendent, was injured slightly, and Walter [sic] Austin, 17 years old, it is feared fatally. The cause of the explosion is unknown.*

The *Plattsburgh Sentinel* followed on February 26, 1886, carrying a more descriptive story regarding the incident; and the *Plattsburgh Republican* followed with its own reporting on February 27, 1886. The Clinton Powder Works was located a mile and a half to two miles outside of the village of Plattsburgh on the south side of the Saranac River and was in the business of manufacturing dynamite. At about 2:15 p.m. on that Wednesday, a violent blast was felt and heard up to fifteen miles in every direction from the works. Residents of Keeseville, Grand Isle and Saranac

Early view of Margaret Street, Plattsburgh. *Library of Congress, Prints and Photographs Division.*

were all startled by the shock. At that time, the facility consisted of a factory—a shoddy, two-story wooden building housing the boiler, vats and other manufacturing equipment—and an adjoining brick building where the dynamite cartridges were stored. The only men in the factory portion at the time of the blast were Superintendent W.P. Foss and Wallace Austin, a young man not yet eighteen.

It was a frigid day, and Foss was on the first floor attempting to thaw some four hundred pounds of frozen nitroglycerin that had been prepared earlier in the day in the dump tank so it would be ready for the next steps, which would have been washing and mixing with absorbents. Young Wallace was directly overhead on the second floor of the factory making shells. Foss's father was several hundred feet away in the stamping house. The *Sentinel* described witness accounts of the moment of the explosion:

> *Shannon Shuters, an employee, was in the brick building, when suddenly he*
> *had a peculiar sensation, and noticed that the glass of the windows seemed*

to be falling in. He made a rush for the door and saw the air filled with a cloud of flying debris, and in a second more, a shaft of iron came tearing through the roof and striking at almost the identical spot where he had been standing….A young man who was at work in the mill yard was knocked over and crawled under a wagon. He says the air seemed to be completely filled with particles of wood, iron, stones and dirt.

The two aforementioned men, as well as others in the immediate vicinity, hurried to the scene to search for the two men they knew were in the factory building. There they found young Wallace buried in stone and earth in the center of the ruins, right where there had been an eight-hundred-pound vat of nitroglycerin just moments before. Somehow, he was still alive, so they raced him by wagon to his father's house on Charlotte Street. The *Sentinel*, in describing his injuries, said, "One leg was so shattered that immediate amputation was necessary. One arm was also badly shattered but may be saved. He sustained many other injuries, some perhaps internal, and yet hopes are entertained that he may recover. The physicians of Plattsburgh have rendered all possible assistance."

Superintendent Foss "had been thrown a considerable distance from the building," the paper said, "and [was] evidently stunned for a while, but finally came to consciousness and walked up to where the men were searching for him, and in a bewildered state of mind, asked what the trouble was." His clothing was torn to shreds, and his face was "terribly mangled." He was rushed to his home at the Fouquet House. Although scarred and suffering a terrible shock, he survived. The *Republican* said he was "unable to assign any cause for the accident, and says he was simply doing what had habitually been his custom."

Fast-forward eleven months…

It was a frigid Tuesday morning in the village of Plattsburgh, and disaster struck again. The children had been bundled up and sent off to school, women were tending to their household duties and men had begun the drudgery of their workday when a tremendous explosion rang out at 8:45 a.m., shattering windows in homes, schools and factories in the vicinity. The *Plattsburgh Republican* of January 15, 1887, reported:

The sensation was that of a heavy cannon shot multiplied tenfold.…The first thought of a majority of people appears to have been that their houses were coming down. But the second thought generally brought a recollection of last winter's experience, and all eyes turned towards the dynamite factory near the Maine Mill, and a dark smoke rising from that direction indicated that the factory had blown up.

It was déjà vu. A mile and a half outside the village, along the south bank of the Saranac River, the Clinton Powder Company's factory lay in a giant crater of dust, having been "blown to atoms," as one paper so eloquently put it, by 1,200 pounds of exploding nitroglycerin, a key ingredient in the manufacture of dynamite. The *Plattsburgh Sentinel* of January 14, 1887, described the cause:

A short time before the explosion, one of the employees discovered that the roof of the building over the boiler and near the smokestack was on fire. He notified the other workmen and a determined effort was made to extinguish the flames with water, but without effect.

Finding the flames were rapidly gaining upon them, they fled across the ice on the river, and none too soon, for in a very few seconds, the buildings and contents were hurled into the air. Those who witnessed the explosion said the building seemed to shoot upwards for a hundred feet or more, and then the air was filled with slivers, earth, stone and fragments of the machinery. The boiler, which weighed three tons, was landed several hundred feet away, completely demolished, while the boiler head was thrown across the river in an opposite direction about as far away.

Where the building stood, nothing remains but a large hole in the ground some thirty feet deep, the ice and fields adjoining being covered and blackened with the debris.

Thankfully, the factory's nearby powder house and case house, which contained huge amounts of dynamite being prepared and packed, did not explode; but the structures themselves were wrecked. The brick magazine, where explosives were stored, was the only structure not destroyed in the blast, as it was 750 feet away. Its door was blown open, but that was the extent of its damage. The *Plattsburgh Republican* described what happened next:

Within two minutes, many teams were on their way to the spot at the top of their speed. The excitement was tremendous, and it was increased by the knowledge which soon spread that the workmen were at the factory, the

Window shattered in blast. *Library of Congress, Prints and Photographs Division.*

general impression being that of course they were all killed. The factory is located about two miles from the courthouse, and the air for more than a mile distant from the spot was completely filled with minute particles of dust which the explosion had caused. Very soon the news came that nobody was hurt and that fire was the cause.

The second explosion to befall the company was three times more powerful than the first, yet incredibly, nobody was maimed, deafened or killed. However, the material loss to Clinton Powder Works, which was uninsured, was close to $250,000 in today's value. And Clinton's was not the only property that suffered damage from the blast. Not far from the Clinton Powder factory was the Maine sawmill and boardinghouse, which lost all of its windows, doors and plastering, as did a home on the road leading to the factory. In fact, throughout the village of Plattsburgh, many windows and "lights of glass" were broken. Even as far as Rouses Point and Burlington and St. Albans in Vermont, windows and doors rattled as if shaken by a powerful earthquake. The *Sentinel* described the effects to the village of Plattsburgh:

The shock in the village was terrible. The general feeling was as if the buildings had been suddenly lifted from the ground and then dropped back again. Many rushed into the street fearing that the buildings were falling… One of the large plate glass windows in McHattie's store was among those wrecked. A number of houses had the plastering torn from the walls.

The kicker was that the nitroglycerin that exploded was to be the final batch. The factory was scheduled to shut down for the season the following Saturday. Undeterred, the company expressed right from the get-go that it planned to rebuild again after the second explosion, but the residents of Plattsburgh would have none of it. Two jarring explosions so close to a populated area from the same company in a single year's time did not leave a warm, fuzzy feeling for anyone in the community. The *Plattsburgh Republican* stated what the overwhelming majority were feeling when it said, "We think the fact must be apparent to all, from the experience of the past, that these works are located too near the town. There are plenty of available places remote enough from human habitations to secure immunity from danger by explosions to all except employees, and we doubt not that such a site will be selected by the company in rebuilding their works." The *Plattsburgh Sentinel* laid out a far more graphic scenario in its tongue-in-cheek response to the question of the Clinton works being rebuilt:

> *If the people of Plattsburgh are consulted, they will not be. It is to be hoped that the town authorities will refuse permission to rebuild. If not, no one can tell with a certainty when the village* [of Plattsburgh] *may be landed among the Green Mountains* [of Vermont], *which would be decidedly unpleasant for our good neighbors across the lake, if not inconvenient for many of our citizens.*

As the saying goes: Fool me once, shame on you. Fool me twice, shame on me. And Plattsburgh was in no mood to play the fool. One month after the second explosion, on February 11, 1887, an inconspicuous note, buried in the tiny print of that day's *Plattsburgh Sentinel*, said, "The Clinton Powder Co. will hereafter be known as the Clinton Dynamite Co. The manufactory will be built on Crab Island, and work upon the buildings will be commenced at once."

BARNUM & BAILEY CIRCUS TRAIN WRECK

NORWOOD/POTSDAM, 1889

The "greatest show on earth" took an ugly turn on a dark August night near Potsdam, resulting in a horrendous train wreck and the death of many beloved and prized Barnum & Bailey circus pets. Two days earlier, when the circus stopped in Watertown, the *Watertown Re-Union* praised the show as being "more than ordinarily good," and of the circus animals, the paper said, "The collection of animals was large, and the beasts looked well-fed and contented....The exhibition of trained animals, including elephants, horses, monkeys, goats, dogs, pigs, doves, oxen and sheep, was a pleasing feature."

The following afternoon, another successful show was performed at Gouverneur. That village's newspaper, the *Free Press*, reported extensively about the wreck in its August 28, 1889 edition. Immediately after the show, three trains were loaded and departed for Montreal; the circus was expecting a large turnout at two shows in that city. The first train, which carried the tents, props and other belongings, arrived in Canada uneventfully and on time. The second train, which contained all of the circus animals and many of the performers, did not. Ever. At about midnight, an axle on one of the forward cars of that train broke. Acting assistant superintendent Frank P. Brown, of the Rome, Watertown and Ogdensburg Railroad, was on the train when it happened and described those first moments to the *Norwood News* on August 27, 1889:

> He says the train was running only at a fair rate of speed, when suddenly there was an ominous dragging and then a crash, followed by shrieks and

groans from animals and human beings. The train came to a standstill quickly.…There was lively work to alleviate suffering, but fortunately only two men were hurt, and their injuries amounted to nothing more than a few bruises. Their escape was remarkable, however, for there were men sleeping in nearly every one of the six wrecked cars. The elephants and nearly all the animals in the train were terribly frightened, and their cries of terror drowned out every other sound.

Brown told the *Watertown Times* of August 24, 1889, "Every possible precaution had been taken by him and his subordinates to secure the safety of the show trains." It was reported that the train was traveling at twenty-five miles per hour when the axle broke, resulting in two cars telescoping and six cars derailing at Clark's Crossing, a rural railroad crossing between Norwood and Potsdam. The *Norwood News* said, "The cars were very heavy and long, and were crushed and twisted in all shapes and piled upon the track in seemingly hopeless entanglement." There was tremendous confusion initially, as one can imagine. One moment the people and animals had been lulled to sleep by the familiar, rhythmic clickety-clack of the train, and the

Barnum & Bailey train wreck, Potsdam. *Author's collection.*

next moment they found themselves tossed wildly about, awakening to the deafening sounds of wreckage, agony and horror. Bonfires were built a short distance from the wreck to cast some light on the scene so that search and rescue could commence. After every person was accounted for, the grim and heart-wrenching task of triaging the circus animals began. The elephants, which had been on the first car that derailed, were not hurt, but they were frightened and understandably agitated—which made their behavior somewhat unpredictable. Sadly, at least twenty-eight of the show's most valuable horses were killed or had to be put out of their misery along with two camels and a mule. The *Commercial Advertiser* of August 28, 1889, said:

> *The track ponies which have attracted much attention have suffered death in the accident, as did the seven thousand dollar stallion which was driven by Mrs. Adam Forepaugh Jr. It is said that Mrs. Forepaugh wept bitterly and would not be consoled when she learned of the death of this horse. The pretty mule which performed remarkable tricks is among the lost. Seven of the eight chariot horses are also dead.*

It should be noted that some sources later claimed that Mrs. Forepaugh's horse, which was thought to be dead, later came to and was loaded on the train with the other surviving horses.

The *Watertown Times* said that the moment news of the accident reached the dispatcher's office in Watertown around midnight, a locomotive was secured, the wrecking crew was awakened and assembled quickly at the engine house, and all necessary gear was loaded to respond to the scene. The paper added, "Operator Frank McCormick was aroused from his slumbers, and with a coil of wire, a pair of plyers [*sic*], a couple of pads and a telegraph instrument, he boarded the train, prepared to establish one of the outdoor telegraph offices for which he is becoming famous. A representative of the *Times* and the *Associated Press* went with the wrecking party." When they arrived, they were greeted by a surreal scene of carnage and calamity. The *Times* reported:

> *At the side of the track were the bodies of about twenty horses, most of them dead, with here and there one that was breathing heavily and occasionally raising its head as if appealing for human help. They had been dragged... some dying from their injuries, some already dead, and others in such a condition as to make knocking in the head a merciful act. In what remained of one of the cars, two dead camels were squeezed together, the life having*

been crushed out of them; in another was the body of the white trick mule, and in the end of another car which had plowed deep into the soft ground when it left the track, were six of the Arabian horses which galloped so wildly before the thousands of people who saw the circus in Watertown only five days ago.

Tied to a nearby fence were camels, zebras, sacred cows and oxen that had survived the crash and were removed from the wreckage. The horses were soon stabled at the nearest farms of S.S. Clark and John Dyer until new trains could arrive. In all, about ninety animals had been rescued alive from the wreck. The Clark farm is where the wreck occurred, and Mr. and Mrs. Clark did their best to accommodate those who were hungry and tired, turning their farmhouse into a makeshift hotel. Mrs. Clark happened to be looking out her window at the time of the wreck and saw the lights of the moving train. The lights went out when she heard the loud crash. She and her husband and other farmers hurried to the scene with lanterns to see what they could do to help.

When the wrecking crew from Watertown arrived, they labored with jacks and cables, hitching, pulling and lifting to remove the wrecked cars from the track and restore the viable cars. Once that was accomplished, the track had to be prepared, as it, too, was badly damaged. Another crew of

Barnum & Bailey train wreck, Potsdam. *Author's collection.*

workmen was ready to piece back together the track under the direction of the roadmaster. And yet a third crew was tasked by an assistant roadmaster to bury the dead animals. The *Times* said, "One by one the poor beasts which had been valued at many thousands of dollars and admired by multitudes of people only a few hours before, were [taken to] a neighboring field. Here an immense trench was dug about 100 feet long by 10 wide and 8 deep, and in this place the bodies were buried."

The site of the train wreck soon became crowded by curiosity seekers in the thousands. Some viewed the burials, some, including women and children, climbed up onto the wrecked cars to look inside and some were drawn by the novelty of a train wreck and circus animals. The *Commercial Advertiser* reported:

> *Barnum's partner, Mr. J.A. Bailey, is at the scene. He says it is difficult to estimate the loss at present, but it will be in the neighborhood of forty thousand dollars. He thinks the loss of the day's receipts at Montreal will be about eighteen thousand dollars, and some of the horses that were killed were valued at thousands of dollars each. Money cannot replace them, for two years are required for training them after the right kind have been secured.*

The cause of the accident, as stated, was a broken axle. Closer investigation of the axle showed evidence of weakness in the iron. Therefore, although there were whispers of a possible lawsuit against the rail company, it could not be sued because the train with the flawed axle was the property of Barnum & Bailey and the rail company was responsible only for providing safe passage on its railroad.

By midday, the railroad track had been repaired, and the circus train cars were moved to Potsdam and Norwood to free up the rail for regular business. The animals and remainder of the show were then loaded onto another train and transported to the Massena station, where they were transferred onto the Grand Trunk railroad to continue their journey to Montreal. After all, as they say in show business, the show must go on.

THE GREAT FLOODS

NORTHERN NEW YORK, 1890

The week of September 8, 1890, may go down as the soggiest in nineteenth-century Northern New York. The flooding that visited the North Country that week caused tremendous destruction along rivers and tributaries and put many lives in danger. Bridges and sidewalks were washed away. Mills and homes on the shoreline were swept downstream. A season's worth of crops was obliterated. And heroes were born.

Before the big finale, heavy rains had already fallen for five continuous days, and the ground was thoroughly saturated. According to the *Watertown Herald*, the "great storm" or cloudburst late in the evening of September 12, 1890, was unprecedented and caught many area residents unawares. In Lowville, Mill Creek rose fifteen feet in less than two hours; with insufficient outlet, the path of least resistance became one thousand feet of Valley Street from its head to the bridge on Cascade Avenue, where it "broadened out over its banks." Roadbeds, sidewalks and bridge approaches were torn up and swept away. Being nighttime, many residents of the banks of the creek were caught off-guard. For example, Balton Rumble, who lived on the north bank of Mill Creek, barely got his family outside of their home before it was carried from its foundation by floodwaters. Rumble attempted to make his way to the barn to get his pigs out but was caught between the barn and house in rushing water up to his chest and was unable to move. Thankfully, he latched onto a little tree and held tight to it throughout the night. Some of his neighbors' homes were also carried downstream.

Flooding in St. Lawrence County. *Author's collection.*

The home of James Kennedy was carried sixty feet from its foundation with six people still inside until it crashed into the old asbestos casket company. His family managed to climb up to the second floor of the shop, where they remained safe until morning. Mills and factories along the banks of the creek suffered severe losses. Expensive equipment and tools were washed away as walls caved in. The *Journal and Republican* of September 18, 1890, described another near miss and rescue:

> *Willie McHenry, an employee of Mr. Austin, had retired, and Paul Sunderhaft helped him to dress. By the time they left the house, the water had raised to such a depth that they could not reach the Cascade Avenue bridge, and they were driven back. Fortunately, they reached a fence post, and a general alarm was sounded for assistance. Steadily the water rose, and despite the efforts of the crowd to reach them with ropes, they were compelled to hang to the post for their lives with the raging torrent now and then dashing over their heads. Their cries for help were heartrending. The hook and ladder truck, ladders and ropes, were brought into use, and when the rescuers were only within a few feet of them, Sunderhaft's strength gave out, and he was swept downstream. The current, however, carried him close to the shore, after going about ten rods, and persons who chanced to be at this point reached him a board and he was pulled ashore. The rescuing party a few moments later reached McHenry, who still clung to the fence post, and he was safely landed on the shore.*

The two young men had been in the current for more than an hour and were chilled and exhausted from their battle, but they ultimately recovered from shock and exposure. In Copenhagen, Deer River overflowed its banks, putting all structures along the river in jeopardy. The *Herald* reported that Horace Ward's sawmill, sash and blind factory and cheese box factory were all carried downstream and destroyed, along with twenty thousand feet of lumber. Likewise, Lanpher & Kyes lost a sawmill and cheese box factory. John Campbell's tannery building was swept away, as was the bridge of the state road and the sidewalks of the village. Between Copenhagen and West Martinsburg, on the West Road, not a single bridge remained intact. Copenhagen, like Lowville, also had its tales of narrow escapes. The *Watertown Herald* of September 20, 1890, said:

> *M. Corcoran went to the rescue of Thos. Bigham's horse which was in a barn surrounded by the rising water. He started to wade to the barn with a lantern, but the water was deeper than he thought, and those who were watching him saw the lantern go down out of sight. They feared he had been carried off by the swift current, and started in a boat to rescue him. Soon, however, they heard his voice inside the barn, and after quite a struggle, he succeeded in swimming the horse ashore.*

Like a knight in shining armor, George Rose rode his horse through four feet of water to rescue his neighbors, Mr. and Mrs. Nelson Gage, from their roof and carried them each to safety. In Dexter, Master Grover Nutting was running alongside his father's mill on Saturday when he fell into the turbulent, muddy water. Luckily for him, Charlie Bloom Jr. was able to rescue him. Twenty-five bridges were washed away in Richland. In the town of Fine, a sawmill and two dams were destroyed. In Edwards, a gristmill, bridge and flume were carried off by the water. Fullerville lost a dam and a wooden bridge, Emeryville lost its new iron bridge to the storm, and the covered bridge in Gouverneur was severely damaged. It's almost mind-numbing to consider the scope of destruction the great storm of that fateful evening caused.

The fairs at Cape Vincent, Carthage, Potsdam and Ogdensburg went on, but they were "nearly handicapped by the heavy rains," according to the *St. Lawrence Herald* of September 19, 1890. The *Ogdensburg Journal* of September 15, 1890, added that a "big washout occurred on the Rome, Watertown and Ogdensburg [railroad], between Mannsville and Pierrepont Manor, the flood carrying away the track…and making a deep channel across the line." All areas of New York State were affected by the heavy rainstorms that week. In eastern Oswego, an incredible forty bridges were carried away, and in Ithaca, the county fair was canceled after the racetrack became flooded in water six feet deep. The general grounds, including the animal pens, were submerged in water three feet in depth, resulting in the loss of horses and other livestock that could not make it to dry land.

The Lowville paper called the disaster "Worse Than Fire," which spoke volumes, considering that fires of that period often destroyed entire villages. Indeed, the flooding storms of 1890 decimated portions of many towns and villages throughout the region. By Saturday, nearly every mill in Lowville was closed, and the streetlights could not be lit due to the high water. Water for the village had been shut off that evening due to flooding, and when it was returned to service in time for Sunday morning breakfast, it was too muddy to use, according to the *Watertown Times* of September 15, 1890.

At Pulaski, the Salmon River had risen higher than ever before, according to the *Pulaski Democrat* of September 18, 1890. In the lower part of the village, twenty-three bridges were swept away. The paper said:

> *Spring Brook also assumed unheard of proportions, and it was only through the exertions of Supt. Fitch, the Mahaffy Brothers, and others, that the Pulaski Water Works reservoir was saved. The spillway, large as it was, could not carry off the great flood of water that came pouring down, and the great dam of clay and paddle work was overflowed to the depth of a foot or more of water. The alarm was sounded, and a number of men gathered to prevent a catastrophe. Mr. Fitch opened the mud gate and turned full force on the water wheel, thus reducing the volume somewhat and undoubtedly saved the reservoir.*

Friday night's storm was not only of cloudburst intensity, but it also was electrical in nature. In Pulaski, J.W. Wood's yard was struck by a lightning bolt that left the residents nearby badly shaken, and it also left a "ragged looking hole in the ground." Sadly, one timid pet in the vicinity died of fear. The *Pulaski Democrat* reported, "We learn that at the instant of the discharge of electricity, a canary bird in the residence of J. A. Blount screamed out, either from pain or fright and fell dead in the bottom of the cage." A hog pen at the Finster Factory at Lacona in nearby Oswego County was washed two miles downstream with nine pigs. Somehow, all but one made it to safety. A special correspondent for the *Pulaski Democrat* told a particularly romantic tale of heroism:

To-day, the 15th, a young lady lost her shawl off the bridge, and in trying to grab for it fell into the river. The crowd were dazed with horror, but a young son of Commissioner Smith, at the imminent risk of his own life, plunged boldly in, and after a prolonged struggle grappled her in mid current, and struck out manfully for the shore. All were screaming and telling what to do, and someone said, "Throw him a rope." One young man, who like the river was too full, grabbed a log chain and threw it, taking young Smith on the head and causing an almost fatal ending of the accident. But Smith rose to the surface and reached the shore with his prize amidst the shouts and cheers of his many friends.

The sheer volume of destruction and personal tragedies made the flood of 1890 one for the record books. The *Democrat* called it the greatest flood ever known in Northern New York, and the journalists were certainly not alone in their belief. The highway commissioner estimated the damage to roads and highways to be tremendous with so many bridges having been washed away. And the loss to property (gardens, homes, mills, factories, farms, sidewalks and so on) was inestimable over such a wide region. But even in the worst of times, hardy Northern New Yorkers are sharp-witted. As they say, sometimes you have to laugh, or you'll cry, so I'll leave you with this nugget. On September 18, 1890, the *Ogdensburg Journal* shared an amusing exchange from the *Watertown Times*:

Speaker Reed is always ready. Congressman Lansing received a message from him the other day to return to Washington. The railroads were flooded, bridges gone and roadbeds washed away in several places, and he tried to explain it in a dispatch which the operator spaced as follows:

Hon. Thos. B. Reed:
   Impossible to come. Wash out on the line. —LANSING.

To which the following was returned:

Hon. Frederick Lansing:
   All right. Then you can come with a clean shirt on. —T.B. REED.

8

THE *HARTFORD* GOES DOWN—ALL HANDS LOST

CLAYTON, 1894

Thursday, October 11, 1894, was a day that will live in infamy for the quaint shoreside village of Clayton. The horrific news of the schooner *Hartford*'s fate rocked the tightknit community. Seven of their own went down with the ship, and the news of the disaster at eight o'clock the next morning was met with disbelief and grief. The *Clayton Independent* newspaper described the initial scene on the streets of Clayton:

> *The meagre details at first received were discussed with blanched faces on the streets and in the various business places. Relatives and intimate friends of the dear ones supposed to be on board the vessel were hurrying about with tear-stained faces and heavy hearts, clinging to the last straw in their hope that perhaps at least some were saved. The cloud that had fallen was a heavy one, and the scene was heartrending in the extreme.*

Thursday morning, the water on Lake Ontario was angry, hostile and forbidding with gale-force winds blowing from the northwest becoming more powerful as the day went on. It was truly an inhospitable atmosphere for any vessel on the lake at the time. But the *Hartford* was out there, somewhere—and it was fighting for its life. The three-masted vessel, en route from Detroit to Cape Vincent, was spotted off Nine Mile Point quite far out around ten or eleven o'clock in the morning, with water breaking over the deck as it pitched and rocked. Witnesses on shore could see the blue flag with three stars on the mast, signaling that the ship was in distress. The violent wind shifted, pushing the vessel toward the shore and the breakers. The captain and

Stormfront over lake. *Library of Congress, Prints and Photographs Division.*

crew determined their lives would be put more at risk by striking the shore than if they could just anchor themselves far enough out and ride out the storm on the water. The wind shifted again, and by eleven or twelve o'clock that morning, the *Hartford* had been carried, like a helpless and unwilling hostage, toward the northernmost tip of Mexico Bay—an area dreaded by sailors. The vessel was two miles from shore, six miles from the little town of Ellisburg and about ten minutes from Mannsville in Jefferson County, when the crew finally managed to toss the anchors overboard. There, the *Hartford*'s crew would struggle to keep afloat for two hours; but their frantic, exhaustive efforts were in vain. And the most frustrating thing about it is that nobody who was watching from shore could reach them safely.

At two o'clock in the afternoon, the *Hartford* sank, taking seven victims to their watery graves. The *Ogdensburg Advance* and *St. Lawrence Weekly Democrat* of October 18, 1894, described its final moments:

> *Three times she careened over and the angry waves seemed to roll clear over her. Three times she righted. Then a sea apparently larger than the others*

struck her on the port side and she went over on her beam ends, and the main mast and top mast went out of her. Before she could right herself, two other heavy seas struck her, and she appeared to be filled with water. Suddenly with one plunge the vessel went down head first into the storm-tossed lake, and the angry waters rolled over her. She had foundered and not one of the crew was left to tell the tale.

The *Ogdensburg Daily Journal* of October 15, 1894, said that "there has never yet been a sailing vessel that has been able to work away from the long stretch of sandy beach that marks the shore line of Mexico Bay in the teeth of a Northwest gale, and the Hartford but followed others of her class that have attempted it. All without exception have foundered or been driven into the breakers and quickly destroyed."

The victims of the tragedy included the capable and highly esteemed captain, William "Billy" O'Toole, forty-five years old, who was part owner of the ship and a resident of Clayton; the captain's wife, Mary Manson, who was thirty-five years old; and their baby girl, Mary Kathlene, who was just six months old. The O'Tooles left five children orphaned: Edward, eleven years old; Anna, nine years old; Sarah, seven years old; Margaret, five years old; and John, three years old. Mary O'Toole had operated a tailor shop in Clayton. According to Dave Shampine's article in his "Times Gone By" column in the November 22, 2009 *Watertown Daily Times*, an elderly grandson of the O'Tooles said that his understanding was that Mary O'Toole wanted to accompany her husband and be the cook. It is said that she asked her oldest daughter, Anna, who was just nine, to go along with them, as well, to watch little Mary Kathlene. But Anna became greatly agitated on the *Hartford* and could not be consoled—perhaps she intuited the doom that lay ahead— so the boat stopped at Cape Vincent and let her off. Other early articles told of witnesses who saw Mrs. O'Toole following the captain all about the boat in his futile efforts, as if she wanted to be sure that, if it went down, they would go down together—she, their baby girl and Captain O'Toole. The tiny body of the infant Mary Kathlene washed ashore Thursday night unscathed but drowned and was taken to the coroner. Hers was the only body ever recovered.

The four others who drowned were first mate Damas Turgeon, forty-eight years old; William Donaldson, eighteen years old, of Theresa; seaman Dennis McCarthy of Oswego; and Farquhaurson, seaman, of Grindstone Island. Two sailors (Richard Seymour and Michael Purcell) initially believed to have been onboard had, in fact, been on leave at the time. Like Captain

Orphaned by tragedy. *Author's collection.*

and Mrs. O'Toole, Turgeon left a large family in grief—his wife, Mary, four sons and two daughters.

According to the *Ogdensburg Daily Journal* of October 12, 1894, "The life saving crew at Sandy Creek started, but had to return for lifeboat and lines, and before they reached them, the boat went down." Public opinion was harsh toward the lifesaving crew, with many residents believing they waited too long or didn't want to attempt the rescue until the water was calm. An unlikely supporter of the crew was the brother of Dennis McCarthy, who drowned with the *Hartford*. He told the *Oswego Daily Palladium* on October 15, 1894:

> *I have followed the lakes for twenty years, and I know as well as any one can tell me, that it was an impossibility for a lifeboat manned by the best men in the world, to reach a wreck five miles away through heavy surf, such as was running on Thursday within two or three hours.... Had the life crew been within a few hundred feet of her, they might have rescued a portion of the crew, at least. But they were five miles down the lake....I saw their lifeboat after it came back from its attempt to reach the wreck....It wasn't fit to attempt a rescue in. It is my opinion that Captain Fish and his men did everything in their power to reach the wreck. There is no occasion for criticism.*

Naturally, there was a coroner's inquest into the matter when the infant's body washed ashore. The *Sandy Creek News* of October 25, 1894, reported the verdict of the inquest into the death of Mary Kathlene O'Toole:

> *The jury found that Mary Kathlene O'Toole came to her death by drowning in Lake Ontario on October 11, '94, by the sinking of the schooner* Hartford *during a gale; and further that we find that the Life Saving crew at Big Sandy outlet put forth all the effort that was possible for men to do in trying to save the lives of the crew of said schooner or the property of said crew and schooner.*

And that was that. According to the *Watertown Re-Union* in its article "Terrible Disaster" of October 17, 1894:

> *Alexander Manson of Clayton, father of Mrs. O'Toole, was at the scene of the wreck on Friday. He wept as if his heart would break....Between his sobs he told to the reporter the following strange coincidence: "It is*

My child! My child! Engraving by John C. McRae, New York. *Library of Congress, Prints and Photographs Division.*

> *fifty years ago this fall since I last walked on this beach. It was late in November, I think and I was before the mast in the little schooner* Hope *of Port Hope. We got into Mexico Bay in a snow squall and were driven on the beach but a short distance below here. It is a strange thing to contemplate that fifty years after I had escaped death on these treacherous sands, my daughter and her husband and her little baby should be drowned here.*

The day after the sinking, many hundreds of people came from far and wide to view the wreckage, but it could not be seen with the naked eye. Divers searching for remains of the victims attested that the *Hartford*'s hull had remained intact as it sank to the bottom. The hope was that it could be raised the following spring and placed in service as a tow barge. Instead, it remains where it settled, upright in forty feet of water, now covered by sand.

APPALLING BRIDGE COLLAPSE

MASSENA/CORNWALL, 1898

It was ten minutes before noon on Tuesday, September 6, 1898—almost time for the lunch hour whistle to blow, as it did every day at that hour. Bridge crews from the Phoenix Bridge Company of Pennsylvania were hard at work on the new rail bridge for the New York & Ottawa Railroad, which would connect Cornwall Island to the American mainland near Akwesasne. As the hardworking laborers eagerly awaited the familiar siren that would mean break time, an altogether different sound instead arose out of nowhere: an ominous, sickening, creaking, groaning, crunching, metal-on-metal sound at once replaced by a thunderous, whooshing splash and a chorus of torturous screams of dying men. The ironworkers had no time to process the fact that disaster was upon them before being plunged into the swift forty-foot-deep water below.

The bridge on the South Channel side of Cornwall Island in the St. Lawrence River near the Long Sault Rapids consisted of three spans. These were each 370 feet in length and were supported by four stone piers—piers two and three, which were supposedly solidly mounted into the bedrock on the riverbed, and piers one and four, which were on land (one on the American side and one on the Cornwall Island side). It was pier two that inexplicably let go, resulting in the cataclysmic event that earned its place in this compilation of appalling disasters. The center span fell directly into the river fully intact. Although they had roughly two and a half seconds in their 90-foot freefall to ponder their fate, the two men working on that section somehow escaped with only a few bruises.

Massena-Cornwall Bridge collapse. *Courtesy of the Massena Museum (Celine G. Philibert Memorial Culture Centre & Museum).*

Far less fortunate were those working on the span supported by pier two, especially those working on the flooring of the bridge, who were crushed beneath the heavy beams of iron. Their bodies became one with the twisted metal as it carried them to their watery graves and heinously anchored them to the riverbed under 350,000 pounds of bridge. The *Massena Observer* of September 8, 1898, said, "Their corpses now lie at the bottom of the river. Not a single body has been recovered, and there is absolutely no hope whatever of finding any until the tremendous mass of wreckage has been removed." The paper described the scene as such:

Suddenly, with no warning, pier No. 2, counting from the American shore, suddenly crumbled and fell away into the torrent and it was followed with a crash by the center and the span next to the American shore with the men on it, some of them at a height of 90 feet. The bodies came to the surface, and the work of rescue began. This was hopelessly inadequate, there being only a few boats in the vicinity, and very few men who would undertake to swim out into the turbulent waters. Many who might have been saved were drowned before help could reach them. Piteous appealing faces sank beneath the waters before the eyes of helpless onlookers. Bodies came to the surface for a moment, and then passed out of sight, perhaps forever. It was a terrible and heartrending scene. Even those who were gotten to land alive were in such condition that many died on the way to the hospitals. Some had their backs broken, others both legs, while others were crushed by the heavy irons.

The tug *Beaver* carried the bodies of the wounded to Cornwall, where they were placed in the hospital. At the earliest estimates, seventeen men were injured (some mortally) and fourteen killed in the disaster. However, the *Malone Gazette* of September 9, 1898, placed those numbers higher, stating (perhaps a bit prematurely):

It is known that 82 workmen reported for duty Tuesday morning and late Tuesday night only 38 of the number had been accounted for. Of the thirty-three victims taken to the Cornwall hospital, eighteen had died by evening, and it is believed that fully twenty more were either killed by the falling bridge or drowned and it is probable that the bodies of many of the latter will never be recovered, owing to the depth of the water and the swiftness of the current.

The fifteen initially counted as having been instantly killed were foreman W.J. Cubby of Paterson, New Jersey; W.J. Jackson of Columbus, Ohio; Louis Baumer of Johnstown, Pennsylvania; R.L. Dysart of Tyrone, Pennsylvania; J.D. Craig of Detroit, Michigan; Patrick Murphy of Toronto, Ontario; Tom Birmingham, address unknown; Dan H. Adhes of Cleveland, Ohio; Frank Lavigne of Ogdensburg, New York; W. Sherman of Cornwall, Ontario; W. Saunders of Baltimore, Maryland; John Clause of Caughnawaga (Kahnawake, Quebec); H. Davis of Pittsburgh, Pennsylvania; Cyril Campbell of Cornwall, Ontario; and Daniel Hughes, whose body was the first to be recovered under the wreck on September 8, 1898. Many of these were found floating near St. Regis (Mohawk Reservation). On September 15, 1898, the *Malone Palladium* said, "Two more bodies were found on Saturday, floating, names unknown. There are several yet missing and are supposed to be beneath the ruins. Later—A few other bodies have since been recovered, and several can be seen through the clear water, pinned under heavy stones and timbers."

The wounded included John Wilson of Malden, Massachusetts; George Bloxon of Perkinsville, Vermont; Bert Brant of Deseronto, Ontario; Peter

Massena-Cornwall Bridge collapse, collage. *Courtesy of the Massena Museum (Celine G. Philibert Memorial Culture Centre & Museum).*

O'Keefe of Cornwall Island; Louis White of Cornwall Island; Andrew Smith of Rochester, New York; W. Thompson of Montreal, Quebec; John Fraser of Quebec; John Bero of Cornwall Island; P. Delahante of Elkhart Lake, Wisconsin; D. Barton of Buffalo, New York; Michael Burke of Johnson, Vermont; Henry Leaf of Cornwall Island; P. White of Cornwall Island; P. Day of Cornwall, Ontario; and Mitchell Reeves of Cornwall, Ontario. A few men escaped with relatively minor injuries, but most suffered serious crush injuries, such as broken legs, spinal injuries and severed limbs.

Finding the corpses of the remaining deceased proved time-consuming. The wreckage removal and body recovery efforts required intensive labor and specialized equipment designed for use in dangerous and adverse conditions. On September 10, 1898, the *Ogdensburg Journal* reported that none of the bodies of the drowned had yet been recovered as of Thursday, September 8, two days after the tragedy. By September 15, the *Journal* said that only three bodies remained buried in the debris. And finally, on September 22, the last body, that of Henry Davis of Pittsburgh, was pulled from the wreckage. By then, a couple hundred people were visiting the site each day to view the destruction and watch recovery efforts.

In early reporting, the cause of the disaster was speculative. The *Scientific American* magazine of October 1898 mused:

> *The terrible disaster at Cornwall, Ontario, in which a river pier and two adjacent spans fell into the river, is a case (now happily very rare) of the collapse of a presumably first class structure which was being erected by well known contractors under the supervision of engineers of standing and reputation. For the reason that the swiftness of the current has prevented any thorough examination of the river bottom, it is impossible to determine, except by conjecture, the cause of the disaster...*

The *Malone Palladium* of September 15, 1898, theorized:

> *The bridge consisted of three spans, each 368 feet long. Two spans were completed. The ties and rails were laid and the painters were well up with their work. The third and last span was resting upon its foundation and some of the men were at work taking out the trestle, or false work, underneath, and it appears that when the pier was called upon to bear the entire weight of the two spans, it suddenly collapsed and carried its load of human freight with it, about 60 men.*

And the *Massena Observer* added its supposition to the mix:

> *The cause of the sudden crumbling away of the pier is generally thought to have been the action of the water on the concrete foundation. There is no sign of the pier. It has disappeared as completely as if it were a card house.*
>
> *The masonry work on the bridge was built by the Sooysmith Company of New York and was supposed to be first-class masonry. The manager of the company, Geo. E. Thomas, is confident that his company is not responsible for the accident. The generally accepted theory is that there was either some defect in the base of the pier, or that the pier was set on what was supposed to be firm bottom and which proved to be only a strata of rock or gravel, lying on soft mud, which gave way underneath the great weight of the iron and stone.*

Well, of course, the Sooysmith Company denied culpability. The material loss alone was estimated to be around $7.5 million in today's dollars. The loss

Massena-Cornwall Bridge collapse after cleanup. *Courtesy of the Massena Museum (Celine G. Philibert Memorial Culture Centre & Museum).*

of life and limb was too great to ever be fairly compensable. If Sooysmith was responsible, it would put the company out of business. On the other hand, the Phoenix Bridge Company began construction of the bridge on top of the pier bases even before formally accepting the adequacy of the stonework completed by Sooysmith. There seemed enough blame to go around. The *Chateaugay Journal* summed up the general sentiment when it said in its September 15, 1898 edition, "There is a widespread impression in this city [Ogdensburg] and district which is experienced in that popular verdict. 'Somebody has blundered,' and the most searching of investigations is demanded by public sentiment. They who planned and superintended the construction of the piers may, it is thought, have to answer before the proper tribunal for their work."

As required by the inquest, engineers, experts and drilling teams were brought in and ultimately determined with reasonable certainty the cause of the disaster. On November 3, 1898, the *Massena Observer* ran a story titled, "Foundation Faulty," which announced that the bridge collapse was due to recklessly installed borings and piers:

> *The cause of the terrible disaster at the Cornwall bridge has at last been discovered. Mr. Douglas, of the Dominion Government, has been at work*

for some time past making soundings in the vicinity of the piers. He has been assisted by Prof. Burr, of Columbia College, New York; C.C. Martin, Superintendent of the Brooklyn bridge; G.W. McNulty of New York; and several expert engineers.

On Saturday last, the Canadian scow and boring apparatus was taken around to the south channel and anchored by the fallen pier. A diamond drill was soon in operation and was working in the hard pan at the bottom of the river. After boring down about two feet, the drill struck into muddy deposit, a kind of clay formation. For fourteen feet the drill passed through this soft material and still no hard bottom was found.

As a result of this discovery, there is little doubt that the layer of hard pan on which the pier rested was insufficient to hold the huge weight of stone and iron, and the collapse was occasioned thereby.

And there you have it. When human nature underestimates or gambles with the power of Mother Nature, we are not-so-gently reminded that we are but mere mortals, in the physical sense, powerless in the presence of natural forces. Had the original drilling gone just a few feet farther, or taken just a few days longer, this terrible tragedy could have been prevented.

TUPPER LAKE IN RUINS

TUPPER LAKE, 1899

A Tupper Lake man named Cohen was having a rough night taking care of his ill wife and was about to finally lay his weary bones down for a few blessed hours of rest around 1:00 a.m. on July 30, 1899, when he heard the distinct sound of wood crackling outdoors. Running to the window, he saw that the shed of King & Page's grocery store on the corner of Church and Lake Streets was on fire. Bolting out the door, he yelled into the darkness, *Fire! Fire!* The verbal alarm in the otherwise sleepy little village pierced the tranquil night and startled the residents—some 2,500 strong—awake. There would be no sleep that night for Cohen and his wife—nor for anyone else living in Tupper Lake. Chaos ensued. Plain and simple. The one thing many had feared could happen was happening. The dangerously cramped uptown business section was ablaze.

In 1899, Tupper Lake was young as far as towns go. Only by the mid-1800s had it even been settled, when it showed great promise for the logging industry—and it would not disappoint. Lumberyards and sawmills arrived, one by one, staking their claims and clearing the land that would become the town. Business thrived. Indeed, Tupper Lake was once ranked as the state's top lumber producer. Then, when Tupper became the headquarters of the Northern Adirondack Railroad in 1890—thanks to the dauntless efforts of lumberman-entrepreneur John Hurd, who built the road that became the New York and Ottawa Railroad—it was the icing on the cake. The little town soon became a lumberman's dream and a sportsman's paradise, attracting outsiders and prospering.

TUPPER LAKE FIRE SWEPT

Almost Entire Town Destroyed Last Sunday Morning.

IT CONSUMES 170 BUILDINGS

The Loss Is About $175,000 with Insurance at Less than $75,000—Every Business Place In the Village Burned and No Goods Saved—Terrible Holocaust.

Tupper Lake is in sackcloth and ashes, mourning because just before daylight Sunday the very heart of her business and residence district was consumed by fire. A building here and there is all that is left of the village proper and the blistered

Front-page headline of August 3, 1899. *From the Massena Observer.*

All the homes and businesses that a growing community would need sprang up quickly in the 1890s—churches, six hotels, large sawmills, grocers, meeting places, mercantile establishments and so on. For the most part, they were built using—you guessed it—lumber. Yet for all the village elders' efforts to set up a proper community that could provide adequately for its residents, they had not yet organized a fire department—nor, for that matter, even a viable system of public waterworks. They had begun planning for such earlier that year, according to the *Troy Times* of July 31, 1899; but the project was not complete, and no pipeline was yet in service, when the fire began at King & Page's grocery. A day after the fire, the *Times* reported, "There is a process of construction of a water system at Tupper Lake. The water will be piped in from Simone pond, four miles distant. This will admit of a volunteer fire department, and with yesterday's lesson so vividly before them, there will be no loss of time in organizing a department."

Adjoining the grocery store, which was fully engulfed in flames, were its horses' stables and the Windsor Hotel. Both structures promptly fell victim to the growing inferno, as would countless others in the next five hours of what villagers dubbed the "Apocalypse." Some news articles blamed a strong wind for causing such a rapid spread of fire; but others, such as the *Elizabethtown Post*, said, "There was little wind, but the flames flew

Fire Scene at Night, by Robert Salmon, 1831. *Wikimedia Commons.*

from building to building, defying the bucket brigades and weak efforts of men without adequate apparatus," to fight such an inferno. The *Massena Observer* of August 3, 1899, described the frantic, though futile, efforts to battle the blaze:

> *Two-inch hose stream from the Export Lumber company's mill was turned on, but it dried to air in the fierce heat of the frame houses. Blankets saturated with water and bucket after bucket were used, but they failed to check even momentarily the flames. In some instances, even these puny efforts were relaxed, and men stood helpless while the savings of years, the homes of their families, melted away like ice.... The flames leaped eastward along Lake street, consuming three buildings and only stopping because there was no fuel beyond. It roared up Church street, making but little moment of seven substantial frame buildings, and then put its fiery grasp on the business blocks on Main street. Until this time, there was hope of confining it to Church street; now all efforts were bent on saving a few buildings.*

East and west over Main street sped the flames, until at one time 30 buildings were burning. By the use of saturated blankets, the new opera house, a rude frame structure, was saved. At the Altamont the women of the house assisted the men and gradually the efforts of the village were centered on saving that hostelry....While the fight for the Altamont was going on, the fire swept a path 200 yards wide right thro' Main, High and Church streets and Waubeek avenue, leaving behind them only ashes to mark the place where Tupper Lake and the country for miles around was wont to do its shopping. Mountain street was the last offering. Every one of its six buildings fell prey, and then the flames leaped into the woods, where the green trees resisted its power and ended the mad revel.

"With the rising of the sun," the *Post* said, "the fire seemed to lose energy, and before the breakfast hour, the smoking ruins of the Adirondack village were safe from further damage from the fire." According to the *Malone Palladium* of August 3, 1899, when a representative of that paper arrived at Tupper Lake the day after the fire, "the scene was one of almost complete desolation."

Heaps of smoldering ruins greeted the eye on every hand, reminding one of some vast forest fire, so complete was the destruction. Not a post or stick of any kind was left standing in the burned district—only heaps of twisted rods, tin roofing, machinery, and several piles of ice that lay melting in the sun. The people seemed to be stunned by their great loss, hardly able to grasp the full meaning of this terrible holocaust.

Within four or five hours, the Tupper Lake fire had consumed 170 buildings in the business and residential districts, spanning twelve acres of land. The *New York Times* of August 1, 1899, announced soberly:

Save two hotels, the Opera House, Catholic Church, and a few straggling tenement houses on the outskirts, not a single block or house remains. Not a business establishment of any kind escaped. The buildings were all of wood, and there being no fire protection, insurance rates were well nigh prohibitive as far as the poorer class were concerned. Thus, hundreds are left homeless and destitute....Men were dazed and watched all of their earthly possessions go up in smoke, while women and children wept and wrung their hands. Hundreds sought shelter in the only remaining church and at the Opera House. Steps are being taken to feed and care for them.

Although there was never a doubt about what structure the fire began in, the cause of the fire was never fully understood. The *Malone Palladium* said, "The origin of the fire is still clouded in mystery, and many opinions are given as to the cause; but that of incendiarism seems to have gained considerable credence in the town, and if it could be proven that anyone had committed such a heinous crime and the guilty party found, the chances are that he would find little mercy at the hands of the victims of this great catastrophe."

The losses to homes and businesses totaled $175,000, which equates to over $5 million today. Yet insurance (primarily through F.S. Chinnell of Malone and Mutual Insurance Company of Ogdensburg) covered only $75,000 of those losses, due to the unusually high cost of insurance and the lack of other reputable insurance companies willing to do business with the Adirondack community. While some who suffered losses immediately ordered lumber to begin rebuilding, others "thought of removing to the junction of the railroads two miles from the present site, and the fire may be the means of merging Tupper Lake village into Tupper Lake Junction," according to the *Elizabethtown Post*. In fact, there was the tale of one colorful character named Fournier who was missing and presumed dead in the fire. However, the elderly man was later seen "going toward the Junction swinging his hat and remarking that he was 'going to quit the town,'" according to the *Malone Palladium* of August 3, 1899. In the end, most everyone decided to remain, roll up their sleeves and rebuild. Today's Tupper Lake proudly bears testimony to the spirit of cooperation, the strength, the determination and the dreams of its earliest residents.

SNOWBOUND

NORTH COUNTRY, 1900, 1912, 1928

This region has played host to countless blizzards and snow events in its history—far too many to list here. Most have not risen to the definition of disaster. That is, most have not resulted in loss of lives, most have not resulted in great destruction to property and most have not caused substantial disruption to a community's daily operations that impeded its ability to recover. Most. But not all. This is the North Country, after all.

MARCH 1, 1900

The crippling Great Blizzard of 1900 brought Northern New York to its knees. March came in like a lion—and not just any lion, but the lion king himself. The *Norwood News* reported twelve-foot snowdrifts on Main Street on March 2, the day after the blizzard. Upon the tallest snowdrift, the paper said, "Some patriotic citizen placed a flag on its summit where it waved in silent glory." Snow removal from the streets required many able-bodied men shoveling by hand—not an easy task with two feet of snow and temperatures well below zero. The *Ogdensburg Journal* dubbed Ogdensburg the "City of the Snows," saying, "It is the sole topic of conversation. Not for many years has there been such a continuous fall of snow in this region." The blizzard, which began early on Thursday, March 1, brought the railroads to a standstill, preventing mail delivery from all parts south. Trains were stalled on the

"Breaking Out the Road," circa 1900–10. *From the collections of the St. Lawrence County Historical Association.*

buried tracks all over the North Country. Efforts of train-driven snowplows coming to the rescue were futile, as they, too, became stuck. At the Heuvelton station, a "gang of sixty shovelers were at work around the depot" trying to shovel out the plow stuck there, where it "ran into a mountain of snow."

It took several days to clear Ford Street and most other streets in the vicinity. The article also stated that of the large number of employees working at the State Hospital, only two attempted to walk home through the blizzard after streetcar connections to the facility were suspended. In some places, like Isabella Street and Washington Street, snowdrifts reached eight to ten feet in height, and in "countless other places throughout the city, portions of streets [were] rendered absolutely impassable for teams and pedestrians." Still, schools in the Ogdensburg district remained open for those who could brave the blinding elements. Needless to say, attendance was sparse. One man named Thomas Peacock, who lived near the "Klondike" planing mills, had a very frightening experience in his attempt to pick his children up from No. 4 school in that city. The *Ogdensburg Journal* said:

> *Yesterday afternoon he hitched up and started for this city after his children, who are pupils at No. 4 school. He left his home at a quarter before 3, when the storm was at its height, and started down on the ice. He had hardly left the shore when the snow blinded his vision and his surroundings*

were shut out from view. Being quite sure of the road, he continued, but his calculations were upset, and instead of driving down along the shore, he unknowingly directed his horse toward the middle of the river. When a half-mile out, the sleigh overturned and he lost his blankets. He started back afoot for them, and during his absence the horse went on. Peacock found the blankets and following the sleigh tracks came upon his horse. There was water on the ice at this point, and fearing that he was near open water where the ice harvesters had been at work, Peacock unhitched his horse and led him back through the blinding snow until he came to a spot where the ice was dry. Giving up all further effort to reach shore, he rolled himself up in the blankets and lay down in the snow to spend the night. He spent the whole night on the ice, and at eight o'clock this morning, found his way home....
His abandoned sleigh was seen this morning about a half mile out from the dock at the lumber yard.

FEBRUARY 21, 1912

It seemed as if spring was right around the corner in late February 1912. The local newspapers described the early part of the week of February 18 as spring-like, saying the snow was melting nicely, boys were out in the streets playing with their marbles and robins had been spotted. Then by midweek, in a complete about-face, the weather turned. It started on Wednesday, February 21, with a brief but mighty midnight thunderstorm—highly unusual in this region in the wintertime. Thunder and lightning and hail and heavy rain pummeled the North Country for a half hour, and several residences in the Ogdensburg vicinity were struck and damaged by lightning. Once that got everyone's attention, the mercury plunged. The now-freezing temperatures, combined with the still-heavy winds and precipitation, created blizzard conditions that lasted for three days and crippled Northern New York. According to the *Ogdensburg Advance* and *St. Lawrence Weekly Democrat* of February 29, 1912:

The [snow]fall in this city was about twenty inches on the level, while outside it is reported as from eighteen inches to three feet, and driven with terrific force by the wind, the drifts in many places were tremendous....
On Thursday and Friday the city was pretty thoroughly walled about. The railroads were completely blockaded, and business was nearly at a

standstill. No farmers came to town, and milk vendors and store delivering rigs had much difficulty in making their trips.

Many trains were stalled along the New York Central lines, and one stalled passenger train between De Kalb Junction and Canton was struck by a snowplow that had been dispatched to help free it. The plow's operator was unable to see the train through the blizzard and crashed into it. Nobody was injured in the collision, but the images show the tremendous amount of manpower required to shovel that train out by hand. Forty locals were hired by the New York Central Railroad to clear the tracks with shovels.

Near the Philadelphia, New York junction, twenty locomotives and four passenger trains were stalled after a freight train got stuck in the snow, blocking all northward-bound rail traffic. Weary and cold passengers were getting off the trains and being hosted at farmhouses along the route until their trains could start moving again. The *Advance* described the scene of the freight train that was snowed in:

> *It got stalled Wednesday night, and seven locomotives snorted, puffed, slipped, groaned, sputtered, and grunted, and the air was blue with the vitriolic vocabulary of railroad men whose nerves had been worn to a frazzle. Seventy- five men puffed and sweated with snow shovels, and soft dialect sounds of choice Neapolitan profanity rose above the sizzling of the engines.*

Train and snowplow collision. *Courtesy of town of De Kalb historian Bryan Thompson.*

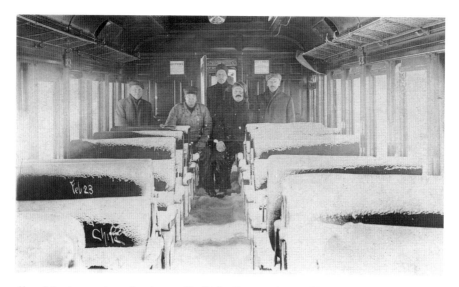

Above: Men in snowbound train near De Kalb. *Courtesy of town of De Kalb historian Bryan Thompson.*

Opposite, top: Aftermath of railroad snowplow and passenger train collision near De Kalb. *Courtesy of town of De Kalb historian Bryan Thompson.*

Opposite, bottom: Hand-shoveled trench for railway passage. *Courtesy of town of De Kalb historian Bryan Thompson.*

Meanwhile, as men all over the region shoveled out trains and cleared the railways in the most adverse of conditions, northbound mail was steadily piling up in Watertown. With rail traffic paralyzed, St. Lawrence and Franklin Counties had not received mail for three days. The *Potsdam Herald-Recorder* described the frustrating situation:

> *Mail trains were lying idle. Freight trains were simply forgotten. Coal was not to be had, except by confiscation. Engineers had to melt snow to fill their tanks, because they could not reach watering stations. The past week has been a battle royal. Business has been practically suspended in all the towns. Country roads have in some cases been closed. Telephone and telegraph wires have been down in all directions. Thursday morning a half mile of telephone poles were reported lying across the Canton-Ogdensburg road. The passenger train that left Massena Springs Wednesday morning got into Syracuse at midnight Friday night with 35 passengers, some of whom got on at Massena and slept two nights on the train, getting their meals at farm houses. Nothing so severe has been known since the famous storm of March 1st, 1900, which buried the north in snow.*

On February 24, 1912, the *Ogdensburg Journal* reported that a train had arrived in Ogdensburg with a heavy accumulation of mail: "The post office was the busiest place in town for the next hour or two, the staff of clerks and carriers having their hands full and then some." Welcome to the North Country.

JANUARY 25, 1928

A terrible tragedy unfolded in Chateaugay during one of the fiercest blizzards this region had seen in years. On a snowy Wednesday morning, January 25, 1928, Gilbert Dunn took his four oldest children to county school No. 12, as usual. The school was just a mile from the young family's home on the Spellman farmstead on County Line Road. The Dunn's son, Gilbert, was seven years old. And a fifth child, only four at the time, remained home. According to the *Chateaugay Record*, the weather soon took an ugly turn, from snow showers to blizzard conditions. Lena Dunn hitched a team of horses to a light sled, left her four-year-old in the care of her husband at home and set out to pick up their other children at school. But the roads were already drifting, and the snow was blinding and disorienting. It was difficult to tell the roads from the pastures in the whiteout conditions. Everything blended together. Mrs. Dunn persevered, though at a snail's pace, and finally reached neighbor John Darmody's home, which was about halfway to the school. She stopped to get warmed up before continuing on, but Darmody took over the team of horses and continued on to the school for her. Three hours later, with the blizzard still raging, he returned the children safely to their mother at his home. He and his wife begged Mrs. Dunn to stay with them, where they were safe and warm, until the storm passed. Travel had become virtually impossible by then. The fifteen-minute trip could take three hours in such conditions. But Mrs. Dunn was determined to return home to her youngest child and her husband, who would surely panic if they didn't return. She feared her spouse would set out searching for them and felt confident she could make it home before that happened.

Around 3:00 p.m., she and her children left the Darmody home with one blanket to share in their sled. The tracks of their sled and horses were covered deep in snow as soon as they were made, the highway had become indistinguishable from the open fields and it was difficult to determine where they were. To make matters worse, the temperature was dropping precipitously, and the horses became too fatigued to go any farther. Lena Dunn lost the strength needed to continue battling both the elements and the horses to get them moving again. Seeing lights of another homestead in the distance, she decided to make her way there on foot and get help, but when she stepped from the sleigh, her feet were already frozen, and she collapsed. Clawing her way back in with the children, she drew them all in closely to her and prayed that help would find them quickly. Gilbert sat on her lap, and she wrapped her long dress around him. Then she spread the blanket out across the others. But it was insufficient for the subzero windchill. That realization came quickly.

The three girls snuggled in tightly against their mother and little brother. As darkness fell, eleven-year-old Lillian "kissed her mother goodbye and bravely said, 'Mama, I'm not going to see you anymore,'" according to the *Ogdensburg Republican-Journal* of January 28, 1928. Moments later, she closed her eyes and was gone, having frozen to death. A sense of calmness and resignation, rather than fear, sets in for victims of severe hypothermia. Once the shivers have passed, the body calms down, as if going slowly into a coma. At this point, victims often shed clothing or blankets, allowing themselves to be exposed to the harsh elements, because their freezing body tells their brain that they are warm or even hot. This probably had a bit to do with the heroic acts of the two remaining daughters on behalf of their brother. As the storm began to clear, the temperature dropped even further, and Ina and Evelyn insisted that their mother take the blanket they had been sharing and wrap it around their brother to at least try to save the most vulnerable among them. Then the four of them huddled tightly and waited.

The night was excruciatingly unforgiving. Just before daybreak, fourteen-year-old Ina whispered to her mother, "I'm dying, mama." She said goodbye to her mother and sister, and then she, too, was gone. Meanwhile, Mr. Dunn was still at their home with their youngest, anxiously awaiting their return. He attempted to venture out shortly before dark but was unable to even find the road, so he was forced back to their house. Then he stayed awake all night hoping and praying that his wife and children had found shelter at a neighbor's home at the peak of the blizzard and were waiting the storm out. By morning, he was in despair and managed to flag down a passing neighbor who offered to stay with the baby while Dunn went out searching for his family. At 9:00 a.m., after wading through drifts in the fields along the road, he found the sleigh with his family. They were just half a mile from home. Ina and Lillian were dead, Lena and Evelyn were severely frostbitten and near death but would survive without amputations and little Gilbert was unscathed. It was a sad time for the close-knit community. And it was a cruel reminder of the power of the harsh North Country elements.

On February 1, 1928, the *Malone Farmer* told of a third death that occurred because of the same blizzard. John Finn of St. Anicet, Quebec, was ice fishing in a shack on the St. Lawrence River near Fort Covington—a common sight in these parts, once the rivers have frozen over. But he was caught in the blizzard while trying to find his way back, like the Dunn family, and his frozen body was found under a mound of snow, where he had collapsed after wandering blindly in the storm. The sixty-year-old cheese maker left a wife and five children.

ADIRONDACK INFERNO

NORTHERN NEW YORK, 1903

Between April 18 and mid-June 1903, the Adirondack Mountains were plagued by forest fires of epic proportions, affecting all twelve New York State counties within the massive Adirondack Park region, from Malone to Lake George and Gouverneur to Port Henry. Anywhere from one-half to one million acres of woodland were said to have been touched (if not entirely consumed) by the flames. One *million* acres.

Strangely enough for spring in Upstate New York, drought conditions had prevailed for seventy-two days straight that year before the fires began, priming the region for easy combustion. Thus, like a deadly pandemic that spreads far and fast wreaking havoc on all it comes in contact with, that first spark—patient zero in epidemiology jargon—landed somewhere, some*how* in the Adirondacks; and it turned our beloved mountains into hell on earth for a few hair-raising, brow-singeing months. It was impossible to keep count of the number of individual fires that sprang up over that period, but some estimates placed the total at well over six hundred. And neither was it possible to determine who or what was more to blame—Mother Nature or human folly? Certainly, Mother Nature had been sorely lacking in the precipitation department yet liberal with her high temperatures and strong winds; but man, too, may have been careless. And we've all seen what the combination of drought and carelessness is capable of (California).

In hindsight, there were probably many responsible parties: campers, hunters and fishermen who didn't extinguish their fires well enough; sparks from chimneys; trains with sparks caused by metal wheels grinding on the

Men fighting forest fires. *Author's collection.*

metal tracks and hot coals falling from the train; careless smokers tossing tobacco products or barely extinguished matches out the windows of the train or from their horse-drawn carriages; farmers burning brush piles, and so on and so forth. The possibilities were endless, and the conditions were ripe for disaster. It was even suggested (though never proven) that some of the fires were incendiary in nature—set on purpose to provide locals with labor. But regardless of the how and why, the people of Northern New York stepped up to the plate that spring. More than six thousand men, with some brought in from downstate to assist local communities, were hired to fight the fires of the Adirondacks. Men (and, to a lesser extent, women) and all able-bodied boys rolled up their sleeves and contributed to the cause, doing all that was humanly possible to save their own villages before moving on to the next one in peril. They considered it their duty to protect their families and properties and those of their neighbors and their neighboring communities. It was one for all and all for one.

Every county, every town and every individual within that broad expanse of scorched land had their own stories to tell—captivating accounts of true brotherhood, perseverance, compassion, strength, grit and survival at a time when communication and travel in the burning forests were difficult, to say the least. Telephone and telegraph wires were down in some places; railroads were impassable in others. Mining companies and railroads were generous in dispatching their laborers to assist. The Lyon Mountain and Chateaugay

Ore and Iron Company, for example, shut its mines down a week into the fires and sent all of the miners by rail to Standish. And the *Pokeepsie Evening Enterprise* of May 1, 1903, said, "Every available man on both the New York Central and Delaware and Hudson [rail]roads has been pressed into service." Quite frankly, it was a matter of all hands on deck, because if the trains were unable to run due to the widespread fires threatening the tracks, then the railroad companies and their employees would suffer tremendous financial consequences. According to the *Plattsburgh Daily Press* of May 4, 1903, a railroad bridge burned near NE-Ha-Sa-NE Park in Hamilton County, so trains on the Adirondack division of the New York Central had to take an alternate route around Norwood. Likewise, a NY&O railroad bridge at Brandon in Franklin County burned, bringing travel on the north side of the bridge to a halt.

From Franklin County came the following newsworthy incidents: In Tupper Lake, the Hurd Sawmill caught fire the last evening of April and was destroyed, leaving two hundred men without jobs. It was the largest sawmill in the entire United States when it was built in 1891. The residents of Tupper gave it their best to save the doomed mill as well as their village and the nearby Junction. (You will recall that their village had also been devastated by fire in 1899, as described in an earlier chapter.) But the fire burned until it reached the pond and lake. By then, considerable damage had been done. Ironically, the women and children who lived in western Long Lake were "sent to Tupper Lake for safety, and the men finally succeeded in saving the village" of Long Lake, according to the *Norwood News*. But they had unwittingly sent their loved ones out of the frying pan and into the fire, as it were. Thankfully, nobody was harmed. As far north as Malone, on the outer edge of the Adirondacks, the smoke was so dense that it was difficult to breathe, and residents could see the fires from almost every direction.

In Mountain View, fire was said to have arisen so suddenly in the back of Charlie Jones's place, setting fire to his hay and the barn, that there was no hope of saving it. A hog, two calves, a dog and eight pigs died in the blaze. And in Santa Clara, the *Malone Farmer* reported, "Rumor has it also that a woman up near Saranac Inn came near burning to death in her little house." The *Chateaugay Journal* of May 7, 1903, contained tragic news: "A farmer, named Burt Esseltine, near Exerton in Brandon, lost a son 15 years old and a horse. The boy went to the pasture to catch the horse and both became cut off by the fires around them and are supposed to have perished in the flames."

One of the worst fires happened on the Whitney tract in the vicinity of the Brooklyn Cooperage Company's camps, not far from Tupper Lake, according to the *Malone Farmer*. The men of the camps were out in the woods where they had been taken by train, fighting the fires to keep them from reaching the chemical works. But when the fire reached a huge pile of dry wood that had been cut and prepared for shipment on the roadside approaching the camps, it went crazy. The *Farmer* said, "The very earth, air and heavens seemed on fire." While the firefighters managed to save the Cooperage Company's camp, General McDonald's camps were completely destroyed, and that happened to be where a young woman became a mother, right in the midst of all the chaos. According to the paper:

> *Mrs. Joseph Prevost, who had given birth to a child the night before, was rescued by Chet. Carr. of the College of Forestry, and another man, and carried on a mattress to the railroad track, where she was placed on a dumpy* [a small, hand-operated rail car] *and wheeled away from the zone of fire, though extreme danger was experienced on the way down.*
>
> *Harry McDonald, who remained at the camps until late, rode a broncho through flames on both sides of the road to escape. Several times he almost lost consciousness and once the broncho fell, but Harry hung on and managed to get through safely.*
>
> *It was at one time discovered that a woman had been left in one of the camps that was surrounded by fire. Geo. McDonald and Carr burst through the fire circle and found the woman on her knees praying.*

The *Plattsburgh Daily Press* said that employees of the Chateaugay railroad were tasked with firefighting duties and that "fully 1,500 men were engaged in checking the progress of the flames." The same article reported, "When the eastbound train over the Chateauguay railroad reached Plumadore last evening, that place was found practically deserted and a fiery furnace. The train was brought to a standstill for a few moments and during that time the express car caught fire and was in danger of being destroyed." While there was no fire at Paul Smith's, the fires surrounding the tract were clearly visible.

Traveling by horse, rather than train, was not much safer. The May 29, 1903 edition of the *Plattsburgh Sentinel* and *Clinton County Farmer* said:

> *On Wednesday evening while a man named Sancombe was driving along the highway on what is known as the Thousand Island road, between*

Exhausted firefighter. *New York State Archives, Conservation Department, Photographic prints and negatives.*

Hunter's Home and Goldsmith's, his horse was struck by a falling tree, which had burned off near the bottom, and was instantly killed. Most of the roads through the Adirondacks are in a desolate condition, having been burned over at least once and in some cases two or three times.

In St. Lawrence County, the residents of Newton Falls feared their village would be entirely consumed due to the speed and ease with which the flames were approaching. So, the Newton Falls Paper Company "shut down its entire plant, sent the entire force, numbering about 350 men, fighting fires," according to the *Norwood News* of May 5, 1903. Assistance was then requested and provided by the Carthage Fire Company, which fought the fire all night. The women and children of Newton Falls were taken by train to Benson Mines for their safety. But many slept in the coaches. And Benson Mines was fighting its own fires; the blaze consumed one man's home, barn, and outbuildings. The *Malone Farmer* reported that two and a half miles from Newton Falls, "the two houses and all but one of the barns on the paper company's farm were burned and the occupants rendered homeless. The families of Frank Manchester, manager of the farm, and his hired man were driven into the Oswegatchie river, where they doused themselves with water to avoid being roasted alive."

Also, in St. Lawrence County, in the town of Russell, "While Mrs. Geo. Bates was out helping her husband fight fire and had her baby with her, they were surrounded by flames before they were aware of it, and, while rushing through what seemed the safest place, Mrs. Bates and the baby were quite badly burned about the face." In Pitcairn, Horace Hurlbut's house and barn burned to the ground, and in Russell, Chester Brundage lost his house and barn. In Trout Lake, a fire burned a hotel and two cottages. Even Jefferson County (adjacent to, but not within, the Adirondacks proper) had its share of stories to tell. Down in Carthage, wooden sidewalks were burning, wires were down and the town and its hamlets were threatened. So crews were brought in by train from Benson Mines and Newton Falls to assist.

In Essex County, the *Plattsburgh Daily Press* said, "The road between Lake Placid and Saranac Lake was alive with snakes, rabbits, hedgehogs and an occasional deer, scared out of the blazing woods." And the *Malone Farmer* corroborated that statement, saying that "from Meadowbrook Farm property, four miles from Saranac Lake, all along the road to Lake Placid everything has been destroyed, and that the carcasses of many wild animals, including a cub bear, deer, hedgehogs and rabbits lie along this road where they succumbed in the heat and flames." On June 5, the *Plattsburgh Sentinel* asserted, "The beautiful Lake Placid country and picturesque Keene Valley are however the greatest sufferers from the present outbreak." While hundreds, if not more than one thousand, men were willing to fight the fires, it was impossible to save the forests on such a massive scale, so their efforts were, instead, concentrated on saving hotels and cottages.

> *The Adirondack Lodge property, consisting of hotel and barns, and owned by State Librarian Dewey, were totally destroyed yesterday. Mr. Van Hovenburg, the manager, and his family, barely escaping the flames....A number of cottages have been burned, also a store on the Rockefeller preserve at Tekene Junction.*

In Clinton County, the woods near Cadyville burned, as did the Catholic cemetery there. The church, however, was saved, but with great difficulty. On the Chateaugay railroad at Twin Pond, a trestle caught fire, sending a freight engine plunging into a gorge. The engineer miraculously escaped with only bruises, but the *Malone Farmer* said the "locomotive lay at the bottom of the ravine in a badly broken condition."

On May 12, 1903, the *Norwood News* said that the fires seemed to be under control (they were not) and that Colonel Fox of the State Forest Commission believed most fires had gotten their start from trains that were not equipped with proper screens in their smokestacks, as required by state forest laws (albeit rarely enforced forest laws with no penalties for violation). Fox based this on secondhand knowledge after learning that Chief Fire Warden Emmons of Albany stopped an engine on the Chateaugay railroad branch between Saranac Lake and Lake Placid for an inspection and found that it had no screen at all in its smokestack. After this discovery, Emmons was tasked with supervising the cause of the fires and ensuring they were extinguished and that there were no more. He ensured that those setting fires during prohibited seasons faced stiff fines. But it wasn't over yet.

The *Plattsburgh Republican* of May 16, 1903, reported that the fires were still raging and that the "fire-fighting facilities [were] utterly inadequate to cope with the situation." By then, Adirondack residents had been fighting fires for three weeks and were completely exhausted. So "the New York Central authorities took 300 Italians from this city [Utica] to the scene of the fire along the line of the Carthage and Adirondack railroad and they will aid the woodsmen in attempting to control it." Even one of the famous Rockefellers was said to have fought the fires burning around his beautiful camp at Bay Pond near Paul Smith's. The elderly William and Almira Rockefeller had been keeping tabs on the progress of the fire near their cottages, and occasionally, William helped as best he could. The *Malone Farmer* of June 10, 1903, reported:

> *William Rockefeller, the multi-millionaire brother of John D. Rockefeller, the Standard Oil magnate, is working harder than any laborer in his employ to put out the forest fires which surround his camp at Bay Pond. His face covered with soot and dirt and his clothing burned from sparks, Mr. Rockefeller is personally directing his men in their efforts to get the fire under control.....No man in his hire is swinging an axe with more vigor or beating out the fire in the underbrush with as much energy as Mr. Rockefeller himself.*

At the blaze's peak, smoke from the many fires (including those in other areas of the Northeast, like the New England states and Canada) reached New York City and even Washington, D.C. On the St. Lawrence River, ships blew their foghorns continually, as there was little visibility in the

Fire awareness efforts. *New York State Archives, Conservation Department, Photographic prints and negatives.*

dense smoke. Finally, rain came in early June, and the fires were put to rest. The loss of property and primeval forest was incalculable. It would take at least thirty years for regrowth to a similar state of forestation. It would take years to rebuild all the mills, cottages, homes and hotels that went down with the infamous 1903 fires. And to add salt to the wound, the towns where the most help had been needed, and where so much had been lost, would pay exceedingly high property taxes in the year that followed to cover the cost of the men risking their lives and battling the flames. The *Norwood News* of June 16, 1903, said the men employed to fight the fires were compensated at a rate of $3 per day. According to the relative labor earnings calculator on MeasuringWorth.com, that would be equivalent to $408 per day today. The *Norwood News*, in a different article, alleged that according to Malone Exchanges:

> *It is a mighty serious charge to make, but it is nevertheless the fact that not a few people believe that some of the fires that have been devastating parts of the Adirondacks were set by men who wanted to be employed to fight them, and so get the three dollars per day that is allowed for such service.*

When the dust had finally settled and it was time for fire wardens' reports to be drawn up and submitted to the State Forest Commission, Colonel William Fox (the New York State superintendent of forests) insisted in public statements that it was all basically much ado about nothing, putting the typical spin on a story that might adversely affect tourism and therefore the economy. According to the *Plattsburgh Sentinel*, Fox believed that "the burned areas are much less in extent than was reported and that the loss in valuable virgin forest has been greatly exaggerated." Furthermore, he insisted that summer visitors would "see no changes in the woods, as he looks out upon them from the hotels, cottages, and camps."

If the state couldn't admit that there was a real problem with forest fires in 1903, what would it take to see steps taken that would prevent a similar scenario from ever happening again? Apparently, it would take five years. In 1908, there was a repeat of the Adirondack fires of 1903. It, too, was called the most catastrophic disaster in Adirondack history. That year saw a dry summer and an early fall. Once again, fires were being reported along Adirondack railroads. And once again, the fires mostly came from the sparks flying off from trains using wood or coal for fuel. The first spark of the 1908 fires occurred on September 9 and was reportedly from a moving train. In five years' time, there still was little enforcement of the laws that required steel netting over the chimneys of trains to help prevent sparks. And now the result of the state's unwillingness to acknowledge the problem would cost it $1 million worth of damage per day.

Two and a half weeks after the first spark flew, the prosperous little village of Long Lake West—which included a dozen homes, a church, an inn and a school—was laid flat by fire in just twenty minutes. According to the *Utica Herald-Dispatch*:

> *Only those who barely escaped with their lives can realize the ferocity of the flames which blew away the town almost in a breath, leveling the buildings and driving horses and other animals in terror through the burning wood. Deer and bear mingled with domesticated animals in the mad flight and the residents who hurriedly boarded a fire train for Tupper Lake witnessed the unprecedented sight of ambling bears, jumping deer, and neighing horses striving to escape the stifling smoke and blinding flames.*

A year later, a series of laws was finally passed to help prevent forest fires, including a requirement that trains could burn only oil for fuel from April through October (the peak fire season) and a requirement that logging companies must take all limbs from the trees they cut instead of leaving them behind, as had been common practice. Limbs left behind would dry out and decay, becoming easy fodder for forest fires, especially in dry conditions. Fire districts were established statewide, and around 120 fire towers were placed on mountaintops and manned continuously to watch for budding forest fires. It took the infamous fires of 1903 and 1908 to get the ball rolling, but safer practices continue to this day to help prevent similar disasters in the Adirondack Mountains.

13

RUNAWAY TRAINS

COOPERSVILLE, 1903, AND MINEVILLE, 1905

It was a warm summer morning, around 10:00 a.m., when James Averill Jr., the president of the First National Bank of Champlain, New York, steered his steam yacht under the Delaware and Hudson railroad drawbridge. The bridge spanned the Big Chazy River in Coopersville, four miles south of Rouses Point, and had been lifted briefly for his passage. Visions of a lovely Saturday relaxing on Lake Champlain put a smile on the hardworking businessman's face. Seconds later, just as the bridge was about to be lowered, Averill bore witness to one of the worst train wrecks in Northern New York history when a runaway train went airborne and catapulted into the river, landing within a stone's throw of his yacht.

The *Plattsburgh Republican* of August 8, 1903, said that the freight train, running from Rouses Point to Whitehall, consisted of twelve cars and "came thundering along at full speed and plunged into the open draw, demolishing the draw, and greatly damaging the central pier, and pulling after it eight cars, leaving four cars upon the track." (Some articles say there were eighteen cars, with twelve in the water.) The circumstances appeared to be in "gross violation of the State law requiring stoppage of every train before it enters upon a drawbridge, and also a strict rule of the railroad company." But there would be plenty of time to lay blame later. The first order of business was, of course, the search and rescue for people and animals. Manning the train were conductor Fred Carswell; engineer Homer Elliott, who was at the throttle; fireman William Braw (some sources spell it Brais), who was in the coal car; and brakemen Kana, Wilson and Frazer, all of Whitehall.

Everyone except Braw—a single young man only twenty-two years old who lived with his widowed mother—jumped to safety a split second before the train went airborne since they were in a position to see what was happening in time. The young fireman, on the other hand, was busy in the coal car and unaware of his impending doom. He was buried beneath the wreckage in the water, and it took some time to reach him. Eight of the train's cars were loaded with cattle, sheep and other livestock, and the *New York Times* of August 2, 1903, noted that "the bellowing of the dying animals could be heard for miles." Twelve cattle somehow survived the wreck, which turned the car they were in into kindling, according to one paper. While the twelve broke loose and were able to swim to shore, the others were all drowned.

As for the fate of William Braw, the *Plattsburgh Daily Press* of August 3, 1903, thoroughly documented his demise, down to every dreadful detail, in an article titled "Splinter Through Head":

> *The body of William Braw, the fireman killed in Saturday's wreck at Cooperville [sic] was recovered yesterday forenoon at 11:40 o'clock by diver James Rogers. Coroner Goodspeed authorized the removal of the body to Rouses Point and the remains were taken to that village.*
>
> *The body of the unfortunate young man was lying close to the pier in the center of the river, under all the wreckage. Had it fallen into the stream further from the pier, the chances are that it would have been ground to a pulp by the dragging of the cars and engine across the bottom in the work of getting them to the bank. When taken from the water, it was found that a large Georgia pine splinter from one of the cars, fully six inches in circumference, had entered his head at the base of the brain and almost protruded on the opposite side near the eye. A large splinter was also protruding from his side.*

Braw's body was taken to Whitehall for burial. The nearest wrecking plant was at Rouse's Point, and a wreck train was dispatched to the scene immediately to see that the track was cleared and repaired so that service could be resumed as quickly as possible. The bridge had to be taken apart and completely rebuilt—an undertaking that would require a lot of manpower. A wrecking crew from Oneonta was also summoned to assist in removing wreckage from the river with large derricks (cranes). The job was expected to take at least several days. Until then, train traffic was diverted to the Mooers branch. Officials of the Delaware and Hudson were not having a good week. The company had crews working around the clock, as it was, to upgrade its gauge on the Adirondack branch. The *New York Times* commented that "this wreck, coming just at this time, causes serious inconvenience." (Forgive me for stating the obvious, but wouldn't you agree that the "inconvenience" was far greater for the poor young fireman who lost his life and the large number of drowned livestock?)

Ultimately, engineer Elliott was considered to be at fault for the accident because he did not bring his train to a stop five hundred feet from the drawbridge, as required. What's more, he ignored signals showing that the drawbridge was open. Yet the train never slowed, according to the drawbridge operator and others who witnessed the accident. It was estimated to be going twenty-eight miles per hour. You can imagine the horror of the crew as they scrambled to jump. The *Ticonderoga Sentinel* of August 6, 1903, said, "Brakeman Frazer was on the running board of the locomotive, making his way to the engineer's cab, and saw the open draw, barely in time to jump. His nervous system is affected by the shock." Fireman Braw never saw it coming before he was impaled. And perhaps, as horrible as his fate was, that was the single blessing in this catastrophe.

Resting place of runaway train in 1905. *Author's collection.*

Two years later, on February 16, 1905, the North Country hosted another runaway train, this time on the Lake Champlain and Moriah Railroad with a heavily loaded engine running from Port Henry to Mineville. According to the *Elizabethtown Post* of February 23, 1905:

> *As soon as they reached a downgrade, Engineer Seward Foote reversed the lever and the brakeman reversed the brakes as usual. This, however, had no effect on the train which dashed on with rapidly-increasing speed. Meanwhile, the engineer, fireman, and brakemen, having no means of controlling the train, jumped into a snowbank soon after passing Treadway Crossing.*

Train No. 104, with its seven cars loaded with iron ore, blew past the dazed crew, building up momentum while going downhill unrestrained for two miles. Then it reached the trestle at the end of what was known as Connors' Y. The *Ticonderoga Sentinel* of February 23, 1905, explained the Ys like this:

> *In its zigzag course up the mountain from Port Henry, the track has three "Y's." The first of these "Y's" below Mineville runs out on a trestle about thirty feet high, and it was from the end of this that the runaway train plunged. The grade from Mineville to this "Y"…is very steep, and the roar of the train, which was going at terrific speed, could be heard for miles. Reaching the end of the trestle, the train leaped through space 250 feet before striking the ground in the field beyond.*

The train was completely wrecked, but no lives were lost or injured. Exactly one week earlier, another train became a runaway near Mineville, but it was stopped before crashing. In that case, a locomotive was going down the hill from Cook's shaft to Mineville, when the engineer lost control of the engine, according to the *Ticonderoga Sentinel*. The track curves around an open mine called "Old Bed" and "21 mine" before reaching the Mineville yard, and it was into that open pit that the train might have plunged, had it not been for the quick actions of a workman at the mine. The train, upon reaching level ground, eventually slowed down and was stopped.

NORTH LAWRENCE IN RUINS

NORTH LAWRENCE, 1907

I n the early 1900s, well before the safety laws we have in place today to protect life and limb, one would expect to read about fireworks-related mishaps in the week following Independence Day. But the fire that devastated North Lawrence on July 5, 1907, was not fireworks-related at all. It began as a tiny spark in the chimney of one of the hamlet's hotels around five o'clock in the morning and raged for hours, unbridled and unchallenged (until the cavalry arrived from Malone). By then, the fire had already consumed the entire business section and some of the residential portion.

It was several days before word of the fire reached any of the local papers, perhaps because weekly papers were more the norm than dailies in those days. By the time the fire *was* reported, it was clear that the story was much larger than initially rumored. Surprisingly, it was a distant newspaper, the *Fitchburg Sentinel* of Fitchburg, Massachusetts, that appears to be the first to mention the disaster in print: "Almost the entire village of North Lawrence was destroyed by fire this morning. The fire swept over the whole business district, destroying two hotels, 10 stores, a number of factories and several dwellings." The local *Canton Herald Advertiser* mentioned the disaster on July 9, four days after it occurred, providing a bit more detail. In part, it said:

> *Every building on both sides of the street from the Rutland station to Robert McCuin's house was completely destroyed. At this point the fire turned and burned to the iron bridge. It was with difficulty that the bridge was saved. The farm house of Mr. Williams, about one-half mile out of town was also burned. Mr. and Mrs. Williams were at the fire. Two small children*

Ruins of Business Section of North Lawrence, July 5, 1907. *Author's collection.*

were rescued by passing neighbors. As a result of the fire, nine families are homeless and with two exceptions, every business place is destroyed. It is certainly a disheartening sight to drive the length of two streets with smoldering ruins on either side.

Unfortunately, as was often the case in small-town America back then, the community had no fire department or apparatus to fight fires other than the bucket brigade. Once the residents recognized the seriousness of their situation and the fact that they could not possibly win this battle, they called on neighboring towns for assistance. Fire chief M.G. Maguire of the Malone Fire Department responded to the urgent plea, bringing its steam engine, one thousand feet of hose and a team of volunteer firefighters as quickly as they could assemble. Although the fire was still fiercely burning by the time they arrived, and the business section was already consumed, they were soon able to bring it under control with their apparatus and expertise, preventing further destruction. The *Malone Farmer* of July 10, 1907, said:

The Malone department worked all day returning at 6 p.m. When the fire engine was taken across the bridge over Deer river, the sidewalk on both sides of the structure had been burned, and some of the bridge planks were burning, but the framework was of iron and this permitted crossing to a convenient spot for pumping water from the river upon the blaze....

Thursday evening the new electric light wires had just been extended from Nicholville and a couple of lights in the street in the business section turned on but now there is no business section to light. The fire is the most serious which has visited a Northern New York town since Tupper Lake was destroyed eight or nine years ago.

What was problematic in pulling this story together is the fact that there were so many discrepancies in the regional newspapers' earliest accounts about the situation. This makes it a bit more difficult in a historical context to separate the wheat from the chaff one hundred years later when retelling these stories, when there are no witnesses still alive to set the record straight. For example, the *Canton Herald Advertiser* of July 9 said the fire began in the Dunn hotel; the *Malone Farmer* of July 10 said the fire began in the old Caul hotel; the *Massena Observer* of July 11 said the fire began in the Union hotel; the *Brushton Facts and Fallacies* and the *Madrid Herald*, both of July 11, said it began in the Dunn hotel; the *Chateaugay Record* of July 12 blamed the Union hotel; and the *Plattsburgh Republican* said the Dunn hotel.

There were vast discrepancies in the estimated losses, with some papers saying $25,000 and others $50,000 or $85,000. One source mentioned later (*Insurance Engineering*) even said $200,000 was being conservative—same with the amount of insurance coverage and the number of structures actually destroyed. Let's just say that it's likely that up to forty buildings were burned to the ground, including hotels, a jewelry store, grocery stores, a barbershop, a law office, the post office, general stores, blacksmith shops, millinery stores, the meat market, woodworking shops, a gristmill, homes and barns. Basically, the entire business section and then some was leveled.

As we've heard so often in such cases in that time period, only a fraction of the estimated losses was covered by insurance. Insurance companies knew of the fire risk to unprotected towns and charged outrageously high rates to cover them—rates that the average hardworking citizen living payday to payday could not afford. In an effort to help alleviate some of the suffering for those who lost everything, a committee of several upstanding citizens of North Lawrence, including the clergy, a doctor, and an attorney, was formed and sent letters for publication to local newspapers for monetary and material assistance. It read as follows:

Dear Friend: On Friday, July 5, 1907, a terrible fire broke out in our village and in two hours Main street was completely wiped out. All the business places, shops and mills have been burned, and the owners who carried but little insurance are practically helpless. Some of our tradesmen with large families, unless a friendly hand is extended to them, will be unable to resume work and support their children.

We the undersigned committee appointed at a meeting held in the village, make a pressing appeal on well-disposed people to send us at once all the money they can spare, and we will distribute it without delay.

Dr. F.W. Crocker, Chairman
Rev. Father A. Saurel
Rev. E.M. McEwen
J.A. Smith, Attorney

That singular humble plea resulted in $1,271 from nearby towns by a week and a half after the fire, equivalent to over $34,000 in today's value. In addition, $280—along with flour, meat, potatoes, furniture, bedding and more—was donated by kindhearted individuals. Had the hamlet invested in some fire protection apparatus—*anything at all*—it would have killed two birds with one stone. Had North Lawrence the means to fight fires on its own from the get-go, insurance rates would have been lower, and the fire might never have spread as wildly as it did that morning. The *Malone Farmer* said it well:

It is strange that nothing had been done by the populace to provide against such a disaster and lower the insurance rate when with so little expense it could have been accomplished. Had there been a fire pump at one of the mills and a sufficient supply of hose on hand the entire loss, with the exception of the hotel where the fire originated, might have been avoided. As it was, every store in the place, with the exception of Mandigo's jewelry store far to the north was destroyed, both hotels, several mills and factories and a number of dwellings and barns.

Later that month, in a special report to *Insurance Engineering*, that point was further addressed:

At 4:30 a.m. July 5, thirty-eight buildings, all of wooden construction, were destroyed by fire in about two hours.

The cause was a defective chimney. Some of the buildings were 3 stories in height. No public fire protection— "…we were greatly handicapped by not having anything to fight with." As to the loss, the same report says, $200,000 would not replace us as we were on July 4.

Indeed.

FRIGHTFUL CALAMITY AT BENSON MINES

BENSON MINES, 1908

Just before the noon lunch hour on Saturday, August 15, 1908, a deadly blast at the Benson Mines iron ore company near Star Lake rocked the countryside and brought the mining community to its knees. At the time, the mining company employed several hundred men—many of them foreigners—and was the largest employer in the immediate area and the only industry. The scene that unfolded in the aftermath of the explosion was nothing short of pandemonium.

Four men—Evangeline King (American) and Harry Boleger, William Dominick and S. Bonger (all French Canadian)—were preparing a sixty-foot hole for blasting with dynamite and packing the explosives with a tamping rod, just as they had done with several other holes that morning. But this time, a premature explosion occurred, killing all four of them instantly. A fifth victim was buried alive beneath the rubble. And yet a sixth man, Joseph King, was thrown into the pit. He suffered a head injury and shock, resulting in temporary insanity, according to the *Journal and Republican* of August 20, 1908:

> *The men who were killed were all grouped about the hole and were hurled several hundreds of feet into the air and their bodies so madly mutilated that identification was hardly possible. Fragments of clothing and portions of the bodies of the victims were strewn in all directions over a wide area....Joseph King, who was in no way related to the King that was killed, was working a short distance away from the group of*

Benson Mines, circa 1890–1900. *From the collections of the St. Lawrence County Historical Association.*

workmen and the shock of the explosion hurled him many feet into the air and he fell into the pit. By a miracle he escaped serious bodily injury, but he was rendered violently insane.

The *Ogdensburg Daily Journal* of August 17, 1908, interviewed several men who were camping at nearby Star Lake when the explosion occurred. They, like many others in the vicinity, headed to the scene to see how they could be of assistance and arrived within a half hour of the blast:

Lew N. Wood, Alexis Schlacter, Frank J. Hayes and Francis Shayne, all of Syracuse, who had been camping at Star Lake, stopped at Benson Mines shortly after the explosion took place in the mine. They describe the scene as frightful. Said Mr. Wood:

"We were at Star Lake, two miles away, preparing to come home, when we felt the shock of the explosion. When we reached Benson Mines the scene was terrible. The mine is near the railroad station, sloping down a hill. The village is close by. From what we could learn, about thirty men

had been employed on the blasting work, but all but a few had gone to an early dinner. The men had put in a charge lower down in the rock, and for some reason the fuse did not explode. Then the men were at work above, tamping in the dynamite, when the explosion took place. It must have been the under charge that went off.

"The men went up with the rocks and were blown to pieces. Two hundred yards away we saw pieces of ribs and parts of bodies. One fellow was identified by his head and shoulders and the remainder of his body could not be found.

"Joe King went up with one of the big rocks and came down again with it, escaping with only a cut on the forehead. He was the only one that escaped. A tremendous rock was blown loose, and the foreman said that the body of the unknown man must be under it, and they went to work blasting this huge rock."

Other workmen were injured, but not seriously, and physicians who arrived on the scene were able to tend to them easily. Quickly news of the explosion and the deaths of several miners reached the village where the families of the workmen lived. Then all hell broke loose, as one can imagine. The *Journal and Republican* said:

A frantic rush was made to the spot in an effort to discover the victims of the accident. Women madly rushed about, tearing their hair and acting in a crazed manner, trying to find some trace of their husbands. The victims of the explosion were all married and had large families of children and the agony of grief and frenzy can hardly be described when the women learned of the horrible death of their husbands. Being of French-Canadian descent, the families could hardly speak English, and the saner element of the community had a difficult task endeavoring to quiet the sorrowing ones.

The *Watertown Re-Union* of August 19, 1908, described the scene in a similar manner:

As soon as the rock from the blast had fallen, a wild rush to the place was made. Women fought with each other in an effort to ascertain any information about the safety of their husbands. When fragments of clothing or the mutilated parts of the bodies were identified, scenes of the wildest disorder and unrestrained grief and emotion prevailed.

Benson Mines workers. *From the collections of the St. Lawrence County Historical Association.*

The Syracuse camping party who spoke with the *Daily Journal* offered their thoughts on the panic that ensued:

> *"After the explosion the town went crazy. There are many French-Canadians there who cannot speak much English, and it was hard work quieting them, but the French priest, in whose parish they were, finally succeeded. People telephoned all over for all the doctors they could find, and almost everyone drove in to learn what was the trouble. The whole county felt the shock, and in the town the buildings were jarred and the windows smashed.*
>
> *"You can judge how excited they were when a photographer arrived and they would not let him take a picture of the mine, threatening to smash his camera.*
>
> *"All the dead men had large families. Bonger had six children, King had seven, Dominick two and Boleger five.*
>
> *"I never want to see such a sight again."*

So frenzied were emotions at the scene that it was thought at one point that an all-out riot would ensue. The *Norwood News* of August 18,

1908, said of the victims' wives, "Their crazed wives are uncontrollable. The more composed people of the community are unable to pacify the women." The *Journal and Republican* described a tense scene that was ripe for trouble:

> *At one time what almost appeared to be a riot was averted when the foreigners, in their unrestrained grief and emotion over the death of their countrymen, threatened violence and at one time the more conservative element feared an outbreak of lawlessness in the afternoon. The scenes enacted around the place of the explosion were very heartrending and pitiful. The foreign element were finally quieted largely through the efforts of the French priest.*

Eventually, as one stage of grief progressed to the next, some order was brought to the scene of the disaster. The *Journal and Republican* said, "The intense excitement and frenzy among the foreign element has subsided to a degree and people are almost prostrate in their grief." The Reverend Father Bergeron conducted a joint funeral service the next morning at St. Hubert's Church. The men were then laid to rest in the Benson Mines cemetery. By that time, calmer heads prevailed, as acceptance of

Waiting for word at the mine. *Library of Congress, Prints and Photographs Division.*

their losses began to set in. Of the thousand people who attended the funeral, three hundred had to remain outside of the church. The *Watertown Re-Union* reported,

> *The wives of the miners attended, with their children and friends. Quiet and orderliness has reigned in the saddened village since the accident at the mines, the first wild outburst and grief and frenzy having subsided. After the explosion the bodies were taken to the priest's house and from there to the church....*
>
> *Work will be resumed at the mines within a few days.*

SEVEN MEET DEATH IN RIVER

GRASSE RIVER, MASSENA, 1911

Shortly after noon on Tuesday, August 1, 1911, a group of residents primarily from Massena and Ogdensburg gathered at the old power house dock in Massena to board the *Sirius*, a double-decker ferry licensed to carry seventy-five passengers, for a pleasant day trip to Cornwall, Ontario. The Massena Methodist Church was holding its annual picnic at Massena Point, and the excursion members planned to return by 4:00 p.m., giving them plenty of time to picnic and socialize. For many, it would be their last such excursion. A terrible tragedy that unfolded in the short distance between destinations that afternoon cut their lives short and sent shockwaves throughout the North Country. As the *Norwood News* of August 8, 1911, said: "A pall of sorrow overhangs all Northern New York as a result of the disaster, which is one of the greatest in the history in this section."

Captain Weston Cline, a veteran navigator of the Grasse River, routinely made two trips daily between Massena and Cornwall on the *Sirius*. He was at the helm of the *Sirius* with fifty passengers aboard when the unthinkable happened near Brewer's Landing. The *Norwood News* explained:

> *The river is very narrow at the point where the crash occurred, and when the bow of the little boat struck against a shoal, the steamer listed over on her side. All those on the top deck were thrown into the water and a panic immediately followed. Several on the lower deck also went overboard and a number of the male passengers leaped into the river in an effort to assist ashore those struggling in the deeper water.*

The *Sirius* before the disaster. *Courtesy of the Massena Museum (Celine G. Philibert Memorial Culture Centre & Museum).*

Women preparing for outing, circa 1911. *Author's collection.*

All but one of the seven who drowned were women. You have to understand how heavy women's gowns and walking suits could become back then, especially when soaking wet, with so many layers of undergarments beneath, like petticoats, underskirts, corsets, drawers and camisoles. If any were wearing the latest trend, the hobble skirt (so-called because the hem was tight around the calves or knees, making it difficult to take big steps), then they would have been at an even greater disadvantage when trying to stay afloat, as they would have been entirely unable to kick their legs.

About thirty of the passengers were in the water and most of them secured footing in the shallow section of the river and waded to the dock. Others, in the deeper part, succeeded in climbing up the side of the boat, remaining there in safety until removed.

For many minutes no one knew just how many were missing and the scene was heart-rending, as mothers hysterically screamed for their children and relatives, and friends sought among the rescued to find members of their party, or to be shocked upon discovering that they were among those who had gone to a watery grave.

Women who could not swim clutched at camp stools and other portable articles hurled into the river by the impact, while others, upheld and aided by male companions, battled their way against the current to the overturned steamer. Picnickers at the International Park, just opposite the scene of the wreck, manned every motor boat and skiff available and aided in the work of rescue.

Many rushed to the scene to do what they could to help, and heroes emerged, as is often the case in disasters like this. Reverend Theophilus Wells of Evans Mills was aboard when the accident occurred and assisted at least six women to safety. John Fregoe (also spelled Freego and Frego in some sources), proprietor of the Albion House hotel in Massena, was aboard with his wife and two toddlers and was said to have saved many lives, including those of his wife and children. The *Commercial Advertiser* said:

Telling his little boy to cling to the railing on the upper deck, John Frego rushed over to where his wife was holding tight to the railing with one hand and clasping her baby, one and a half years old, with a vice-like grip in the other. It was several seconds before Frego could pry the child from the half senseless woman. He carried it back to the other son, aged 3, and told him to hang tight to his brother. When Frego returned to rescue his wife, a hand and hat were the only signs of Mrs. Frego visible above water. After pulling her up on deck, Frego returned to the life saving, clutching waving hands as their owners sank beneath the water. He saved more than fifteen by this method.

The *Advertiser* also reported that "one woman out of sheer gratitude for his rescue of her baby threw her arms about his neck and kissed him." Fregoe, Reverend Wells, Charlie Williams of Massena and A.J. McIntosh of Ogdensburg (who happened to be at a farm near the scene of the accident) were all credited with rescues that day. Indeed, the *Journal* said that "all of the men acted bravely and did everything possible to save the women and children." They were unable to save them all, but the death toll would have been four times greater were it not for those honorable gentlemen and their heroic efforts. The drowned were placed on W.H. Cubley's steam yacht, the *Cub*, and taken to Massena.

Of the six female drowning victims, two were highly esteemed sisters from Ogdensburg: Hattie Parker, age forty-one, and Nellie Parker, age forty-three. Hattie was a bookkeeper and cashier, and Nellie was a beloved schoolteacher. The two lived together in their late mother's house on Hamilton Street for five years and were on a weeklong vacation to Massena, where they visited Massena Springs and planned to meet some of their friends from Ogdensburg in Massena later that evening. The women decided they wanted a "ride on the river," so they joined the fateful Sunday school excursion on the *Sirius*. They sank together to the bottom of the river, pinned beneath the railings, and were found with arms intertwined. Two days later, the sisters—called "young women of sterling Christian virtues" by their hometown paper, were laid to rest in a double funeral at the First Methodist Episcopal Church in Ogdensburg.

Ada Dewey of Massena was forty-one years old and an assistant librarian at the Massena Public Library. Mary Dulash was a Hungarian woman living in Massena. Mrs. E.E. Frith of Maxville, Ontario, was on her way to visit her sister, Mrs. F.M. Bayley of Massena. Frances Frego of Massena, the daughter of J.H. Frego, had boarded the *Sirius* with her sister Addie at Brewer's Landing—the fateful pitstop the ferry made on its voyage to Cornwall. The only male victim was a seven-year-old boy named Floyd Hackett. He was the son of Bert Hackett of Massena Springs and was on the boat with his mother, but she was unable to grab him before he went under.

Captain Cline wasted no time in preparing a statement to set the record straight before the rumor mill reached the steamboat authorities in Oswego. He said:

> *The steamship* Sirius, *a small passenger boat, 62 feet long and 12 foot beam, running between Massena and Cornwall, capsized in the Grasse river at a point six miles below the power house at 2:45 p.m., August 1. There were fifty-five passengers on board, mostly women, and after landing at a small dock the boat listed and the passengers all went to one side. A panic ensued. All those who remained on the boat were saved; those who jumped from the stern or into the deep water were drowned, except the captain's son.*
>
> *As we were rounding to from the shoal water into the current, the boat tipped. I gave the engineer the bells, but before anything could be done, the boat was swamped. While tipping, we drifted some 100 feet and we landed on a shoal. The current threw the bow about so that at present the boat is pointing in almost a direct line from bank to bank.*

What happened next had as many versions as there were witnesses. Of course, there was the captain's version, relayed in his statement. But some sources, like the *Ogdensburg Journal* of August 2, 1911, said the people on the boat scooted to the opposite side all at once to get out of the sun, as the *Sirius* turned sharply away from Brewer's Point, which caused loss of equilibrium to the vessel; and that, combined with the current, which was rather swift at that point, caused the *Sirius* to list to the heavy side and sink. The captain, when he realized what the shift in weight would do, called out to the passengers to remain still, but it was already too late. He then ordered the two little lifeboats lowered by his crew to pick up those who had jumped into the water. The *Journal* added:

> *Practically all of the passengers were on the upper-deck and when the boat started to go over many of them rushed back to the other side. Mrs. Raymond was sitting alongside the rail between the Misses Parker. The moment the boat started to careen she sprang to her feet and exclaimed to her companions, "The boat is tipping." She then hurried over to the other side. The Parker sisters remained where they were. Reaching out, they grasped the railing and when the boat went over, they went with it. When their bodies were recovered, they were still clinging to the railing of the boat.*

The *Malone Farmer* said the boat stopped to take on a few passengers at Brewer's Point when it "struck a shoal about ten rods below the dock and began to rock. The people became frightened and ran from one side to the other, and all on the upper berth were finally thrown into the water."

The *Sun* of Fort Covington, dated August 3, 1911, offered this eyewitness version from the father of one of the victims and one of the survivors:

> *Standing on the wharf, Misses Addie and Frances Frego kissed their father and he waved to them, laughing as the boat nosed out into the current, which is counted on to turn the steamer without other power, except for a bit to give her steerage way.*
>
> *He saw the boat swing into midstream and heard someone cry: "Oh, look, here's a muskrat," and then with trepidation saw the passengers stampede to the port side of the boat. Under the weight, the steamer, with its natural listing, battled with the current, rocked drunkenly for an instant and then keeled over. Mr. Frego sank to his knees on the dock. "Come for me in a boat, oh come for me," he shouted.*
>
> *Mr. Frego saw his daughter [Frances] for a moment clinging to the rail of the steamer and then disappearing beneath the surface.*

The *Ogdensburg Advance* added this questionable tidbit to Frannie Frego's fate: "Just before she went down, she waved her hand in farewell to those upon the sand bar." Now, one could assume such an act was a courageous young girl's swan song, or one could assume the poor child was flailing and trying to get the attention of those watching her from the sandbar.

There were harrowing tales of survival, as well. Mrs. W.H. English was the wife of the pastor of the Methodist Church, and she was taken from the water unconscious but was brought back to life. A young mother, Florence Dowe of Massena, managed to hold on to both of her babies, ages two and four, miraculously keeping their faces above water, while bobbing up and down in the water herself, trying to find the footing to make it to shore in water that was just over her head. Never underestimate the determination of a mother protecting her children. The *Ogdensburg Advance* said that the depth of water where the boat sank was only about ten feet, and two feet of the boat was left protruding from the water. Less than fifteen feet away was a large sandbar, where most of the survivors made their way to safety. Others clung to the portion of boat still visible above water until they were rescued.

Ironically, on August 3, 1911, two days after the *Sirius* went down, Captain Cline's ad appeared in the *Massena Observer* by oversight, one can only hope:

The *Sirius* after the disaster. *Courtesy of the Massena Museum (Celine G. Philibert Memorial Culture Centre & Museum).*

"Commencing June 10, and during the season until further notice, the Steamer Sirius will make Two Trips Daily except Sundays between Massena and Cornwall."

While some thought criminal proceedings could be sought, the general belief overall was that the captain and his crew could not be blamed and were helpless "in the grip of six mile currents and the frenzied movements of the passengers, which combined to founder the boat." The accident, while terribly tragic, was eventually deemed unavoidable in the coroner's investigation. And what became of Captain Cline? Less than a week after the tragedy, he was running a different vessel on the same route as the *Sirius*, twice a day. He planned to raise the *Sirius*, make some minor alterations and continue using it again, but the ill-fated vessel broke in two as it was raised from the river, so that plan was abandoned. The *Commercial Advertiser* of May 21, 1912, said the captain had purchased a new steamer called the *Venus*, with a slightly larger carrying capacity than the *Sirius*, and continued running his usual route.

THOUSAND ISLAND PARK IN RUINS

THOUSAND ISLAND PARK, 1912

O n July 9, 1912, a devastating fire swept through Thousand Island Park, which was bustling with summer tourists, and destroyed or damaged the massive Columbian Hotel, the Wellesley Hotel, some two hundred cottages and the entire business block. Though the flames spread rapidly and panic ensued, incredibly, there was no loss of life or grievous injuries. There were, however, many instances of fainting, due to the intense heat of a massive fire on a hot summer day. The loss to property was tremendous—equivalent to a whopping $13 million in today's value.

Thousand Island Park is a hamlet in the town of Orleans overlooking the St. Lawrence River in Jefferson County. There were only thirty-one residents living there year-round in 2010, according to census data, but there were well over three hundred residences and cottages for seasonal use. In 1875, Reverend John Ferdinand Dayan decided that the site would be a great location for a nonsectarian summer camping retreat with a distinct Methodist approach. The Camp, as it was initially called, became today's Thousand Island Park. It consisted of one thousand acres of prime property on the southwest end of Wellesley Island. At that time, families would arrive and put up tents, but the popularity of the beautiful campsite on the St. Lawrence River grew rapidly, requiring additional lodging, which came in the form of the Thousand Island Park Hotel, built in 1883. That hotel lasted until 1890, when it was destroyed by a fierce fire that also consumed many cottages. All were quickly rebuilt, and then some.

The immense Columbian Hotel replaced the Thousand Island Park Hotel two years later. Soon there were stores, a library, a yacht club, public swimming facilities and a golf course, as well as every other amenity one would expect in a resort town, except its own fire department or adequate firefighting apparatus. In 1903, another large hotel, the Wellesley, opened. By then, Thousand Island Park was one of the most popular St. Lawrence River resort destinations. Through the busy summer season, all accommodations were typically full. Business was booming. Then came the unforgettable, and in some ways irrecoverable, summer of 1912.

The fire of July 9 originated in H.H. Haller's Department Store in the annex of the Wellesley House hotel, which was located directly behind the Columbian. It was discovered at 1:13 p.m. by Joseph Rothchild. The store was locked up while the owner attended a funeral in the Thousand Island Park chapel, so Rothchild sprinted to the chapel to inform the owner and sound the alarm. He and several men returned and broke in the door; they called for more help when they realized they could not control the blaze. Although many summer residents hurried to help, and all of the fire extinguishers that

Columbia Hotel, Thousand Island Park. *Library of Congress Prints and Photographs Division.*

could be found were brought to the scene to fight the fire, it was of no use. They had only one hose to aim at the fire, which was grossly inadequate. Meanwhile, a warm west wind had developed that balmy afternoon, and it carried the out-of-control flames quickly through the resort. The *Middletown Daily Times-Press* of July 10, 1912, said:

> *A strong wind which was blowing spread the flames until in a moment neighboring stores were in flames. Every effort was made by the residents to check the flames, but all in vain. A telephone alarm was immediately sent to both Alexandria Bay and Clayton.*
>
> *About a half hour after the starting of the fire, the Columbian hotel was in flames. So quickly did the fire spread, the Columbian was soon in ruins, the New York State education building had been burned to the ground and the post office, church, and all the leading business places destroyed. With the catching of the Wellesley [Hotel] the fire spread throughout the entire park. Two hundred cottages and boarding houses were quickly consumed, and numbers of persons are practically homeless.*

By the time adequately equipped firefighters arrived, the fire had spread over such a wide area that it was beyond their ability to bring it under control. Between the high temperature of the day and the intense heat of such a widespread fire, they were unable to stand for long without risk of collapse. A few firemen thought that perhaps if they wrapped themselves in soaking wet tablecloths from the Columbian Hotel dining room they could last longer while battling the blaze and trying to keep it from spreading any further. But even that effort quickly proved ineffective to such heat. The only thing that would ultimately stop the fire in its entirety was its imminent introduction to the water of the St. Lawrence River, which was where it was headed. With little more to do than water down the ruins, the firefighters and residents watched the fire spread for more than eight hours, consuming nearly all in its path. The *Commercial Advertiser* of July 16, 1912, described it:

> *The scenes among the people driven frantic by the excitement was pitiable. Women fainted from the intense heat, men dropped in their tracks while carrying out furniture and other valuables from the cottages in the vicinity of the place where the fire started. The whole block back of the Columbian was a roaring furnace in less than fifteen minutes after the fire started.*

Fireman carrying unconscious girl. *Author's collection.*

The Wellesley House hotel, though badly damaged where the blaze began, fared far better than the buildings that followed. It could at least be repaired. The Columbian couldn't. The *Advertiser* said the "gables on the rear of the structure caught first and the big frame structure of 220 rooms was soon a seething cauldron of flame and smoke." Everyone had already vacated the hotel, thanks in part to a beloved elderly woman called "Grandma Tousey." The paper said the ninety-two-year-old was one of the cooler heads that prevailed that day and she "stood calmly by and directed the efforts of the younger people, urging them to save everybody from harm before they made any effort to save property." As men dragged items, which meant little, in the scope of things, especially to a near-centenarian; as children ran about crying and searching for their parents; and as women fainted from excitement, fear or unbearable heat, Grandma Tousey offered calm advice and compassion. She even had the presence of mind to check out the nearby cottages for herself and make sure her neighbors were out. In one, according to the *Advertiser*, she found Mrs. Nunn and Mrs. Sager passed out from smoke inhalation and called for help—thus preventing two likely fatalities from occurring.

There were several other close calls, like the firefighter who passed out for two hours from heat exhaustion and the Thousand Island Park Association bookkeeper whose hands were blistered as he gathered all of his books from the treasurer's office. Considering the many, many people directly affected by and present at the fire, it's truly a miracle that nobody was hurt worse. Call it the power of prayer on consecrated ground. The Wellesley was repaired, and cottages were reconstructed, but the Columbian Hotel would not be rebuilt. Instead, there was a shift back to the family resort the park had been, with homes and cottages, rather than the increasingly commercialized path the park had been on. After the Wellesley closed in the mid-1950s, the tourist traffic at Thousand Island Park quieted even more. Today, the park is recognized by the National Register of Historic Places as a historic district. The stewards of the property, the Thousand Island Park Landmark Society, are doing a noble job maintaining the area and retaining its historical essence for future generations to enjoy.

HOTEL FIRE CLAIMS SEVEN LIVES

MALONE, 1913

Shortly after one o'clock on Thursday morning, April 17, 1913, an explosion—or what some within the De Wilson Hotel recalled as the sound of something thumping heavily down the stairs—was heard by those still awake near the corner of Catherine and Main Streets in Malone. Hotel manager William Bailey had just settled into bed for the night when he heard the loud boom from below and ran downstairs to the office and barroom area in his pajamas. There he discovered heavy smoke and a blaze in the barroom. He turned on the water faucets and raced back to his room to alert his wife, Mary, to get out of the building. Then he ran through the doomed building, yelling *Fire!*, doing his best to alert as many of the forty guests and boarders as he could to wake up and get out. But within just a couple minutes, he found himself trapped on the second floor and had to jump.

The old De Wilson Hotel (also called the Hotel Wilson) was going down, and the flames were spreading furiously. By the time firemen arrived, there was little hope that anyone who remained inside the raging inferno could still be alive. It happened that fast. The *Essex County Republican* of April 25, 1913, said:

> The fire apparatus refused to work in a proper manner, it is asserted, and the alarm of 44, one of the most important in the city, rang but once. The firemen were summoned by phone, however, and at once made their way to the scene, only to find it impossible to stem the flames, confining their efforts to the task of keeping the nearby buildings, some of them Malone's most modern business structures, from destruction.

L'Incendie by Alexandre Antigna, circa 1850. *Wikimedia Commons*.

Fifteen minutes after the fire had begun, the walls began to collapse—three side walls caved into the basement and the front wall toppled out into the street—and the roof came down on top of the smoldering rubble. There were no ladders or fire escapes—a regret seen repeatedly in those days before fire and building codes, but to what end? The owners, William and Mary Wilson, had reportedly been warned several times by the inspector to provide suitable means of escape, in case of just such a disaster, but allegedly failed to do so. Now they found themselves in dire need of escaping their own firetrap. How many lives needed to be cut horrifically short before property owners and village officers would do the right thing and ensure the safety of their residents and patrons over the cost of a proper and effective means of egress?

The De Wilson was made entirely of wood, with sheet-iron panels on the outside walls. Whether this was done to give an updated appearance to a weathered structure, protect against rodents, preserve the wood or provide added insulation from the elements doesn't matter. Those particular construction materials together effectively turned the three-story hotel into a three-story wood stove in this hellish scenario. The sheet iron hindered the ability of firemen to extinguish the flames as quickly as they otherwise might have been able to. The *Syracuse Herald* of April 17, 1913, described it aptly, saying the hotel "burned like a paper tent."

There was obviously a complete loss of property, half of which was covered by $10,000 in insurance from the Dudley & Edwards agency, but that loss was miniscule compared to the loss of life and the shock and injuries suffered by the survivors and their rescuers. Seven people met a horrible,

horrible fate—a horrible and *preventable* fate. Others were seriously injured. And the rest were burdened with memories and nightmares of that awful night for the rest of their lives. All of those on the third floor, except for the two who jumped and were seriously injured, were trapped after the stairs collapsed and lost their lives. Those on the first and second floors who hadn't heard Mr. Bailey were awakened by the fire engine and commotion on the street and were able to escape through windows. Several people on those floors were rescued by firefighters and other boarders. Every victim of the fire, dead or alive, had his own unique, appalling story of that horrific night.

Albert Robideau, a forty-four-year-old widower and Malone native who was boarding at the De Wilson Hotel, conducted a café on Mill Street. He retired to his room just a short time before the fire began. The *Chateaugay Record* of April 18, 1913, said, "Robideau was seen in and about the building during the progress of the fire, when he was making valiant efforts to rescue those who were in danger. It is said that he ran all through the house shouting *Fire!* and assisted many to reach a place of safety but stayed inside too long and was overcome by smoke. His body was found on a bed, his head being pinned down by a partition which had fallen across his neck." Nobody was able to come to the aid of the man who spent his last moments rescuing others. He was a true hero and was buried in Notre Dame Cemetery, Malone.

Fred Trucheon was the bartender at the De Wilson Hotel. He lived in Malone with his mother and was unmarried. The *Malone Farmer* of April 23, 1913, said he had "jumped from an upper window while wrapped in flames [and] was badly burned and his back so seriously injured that he died within a few hours after being taken to his home." The *Syracuse Herald* said he was "horribly roasted before he jumped from a window on the second floor. The jar of his impact with the pavement shook the burned flesh from his frame, and it dangled as he was carried to a nearby building." David Schryer, a well-known contractor from Burke, was an overnight guest staying in room 11 on the second floor. When he found the flames coming up the stairs, he returned to his room and climbed out the window, grabbing ahold of a wire that he then slid down. Another hero, he was said to be the first to get out and immediately began rescuing others. He found Trucheon laying in the alley, where he had landed. The paper said, "Mr. Schryer picked him up and rolled him in the road till the flames were extinguished then carried him away from the burning building." Identification was made only by a diamond pin Trucheon wore. He left behind a young daughter, Helen, a pupil at St. Joseph's Academy, and was survived by his mother, six brothers, two sisters, a half brother and a half sister. Like Robideau, Trucheon was also buried in Notre Dame Cemetery, Malone, that Saturday.

Antonio Nicolini, forty-five, was an Italian harpist from New York City who had spent many summers in the Adirondacks and Adirondack foothills entertaining North Country residents. His young partner, John Naola, a violinist also from the city, was with him the night of the fire. They initially escaped by jumping out a window, but then, against Naola's pleas, Nicolini dashed back into the building to retrieve his valuable harp from the dining room where he had left it just hours before. With that one hasty decision, his fate was sealed. His lifeless body was returned to New York by train. The *Farmer* said, "The remains of Nicolina's harp were valueless and spoke mutely of the fate of the harpist who had charmed many while sweeping its strings." As for Naola, who spoke very little English, his face and hands were badly burned, and the *Farmer* said:

> *He was so greatly excited for a couple of days that it was feared he would lose his mind. He was taken to the Smith House where he was cared for and given a suit of clothes. He has since been* [given a ticket] *to his home in Brooklyn, having lost his money, his violin worth several hundred dollars, and other effects.*

The young man had no friends, other than Nicolini, or family in this country; and much sympathy was felt for him. Naola's violin was eventually found in its satchel barely scathed in the ruins, along with a few original and irreplaceable compositions he had written, and they were undoubtedly returned to him. It's believed he threw the satchel out the window before he jumped, saving his livelihood and himself.

Philip O'Connor, sixty-five, of Piercefield, was an employee of the Saranac Inn who had been on vacation for a few weeks and was returning to Saranac when he decided to stop in Malone for the night to get some sleep. He left three sons and two daughters and was survived by four sisters and two brothers. His remains were taken to his brother's (Jerry O'Connor) home in Constable, New York, for the funeral and burial next to his wife and daughter, who predeceased him.

Michael W. Cooney was a former Westville farmer and resident of Malone. He had once owned and operated a livery stable on Catherine Street in Malone and had done road work for the state. He booked a room at 10:00 p.m. that fateful night and went directly to his room to sleep. His body was found in the smoldering rubble, partially dressed, and it seemed apparent that he attempted to leave his room and seek safety but was overcome. His funeral services were held in Fort Covington.

John Moss was a carpenter from Albany, New York, who had been working for several months on the Deaf Mute School buildings. His body was not found until nearly twelve hours after the fire began and was burned beyond recognition. His two brothers arrived from Albany with the unenviable task of trying to identify their loved one's remains, which they were able to accomplish from the gold fillings in Moss's teeth, as well as other evidence found amid his remains. They returned to Albany by train with his body to allow his grieving wife, daughter and father to provide a proper burial.

John Timmons, fifty, and formerly of the town of Skerry, was an unmarried "well-known Malone carpenter, who was working on Gardner's house and had left the home of his brother Fred, to board at the hotel only a few days earlier in order to be nearer to his work," according to the *Malone Farmer*. His badly burned body was discovered as soon as firemen were able to get inside. One of Timmon's five brothers identified him by a pocketknife lying near his remains and "the laundry mark on the shirt band found on his body." He was buried the next morning in the St. Joseph's Cemetery in Malone.

Florence Martin was a Malone native who had been living and working in Montreal as a vaudeville performer. With no other means of escape from the third floor, she leaped out the window in her nightgown. Mr. Schryer discovered her unconscious and lying where she landed, and he carried her to the other side of the street. The *Syracuse Herald* of April 17, 1913, said that she "landed on a lumber pile, and it smashed her into a limp and bloody form." She had been badly burned in the face and neck and had several broken bones in her arms and shoulders. When she came to, she was screaming, as anyone would be in her position.

An elderly Malone resident named Mr. Lee was found by Schryer upon opening a side door to the hotel. Lee was nearly unconscious and suffering from smoke inhalation. Schryer, running on pure adrenalin that evening, seemed to have superhuman strength, as he carried body after body, including Lee's, to safety. Lee revived after being removed from the doorway and was fine. Schryer then asked Lee for his overcoat, which Lee held under his arm, so they could wrap it around Miss Martin's shoulders, since she was wearing only her nightgown and was shaking from her injuries, fear, and the cold night air.

Cora Provost of Ellenburgh was the hotel cook, and she was dropped from a third-floor window, snapping the femur of both legs—a horrendously painful injury. She and Florence Martin were taken to the nearby Morgan's

Barbershop, where doctors were waiting to treat them and transfer them to the Ogdensburg City Hospital by train. The *Chateaugay Record* of April 18, 1913, said the condition of Martin and Provost "was considered as most serious, and grave apprehension [was] being felt as to their recovery." Dr. Madill, who was caring for the women in Ogdensburg, said he believed they would both survive, but their recovery would take many months.

Others who escaped by jumping onto the roof of an adjoining building suffered various, non-life-threatening injuries. Nelson Gildie and Edward Frechette suffered minor burns; C.D. Parlow's feet were injured by the burning floors, but he still managed to jump; Fred Bruseau, who worked at the Star Theatre, injured his knee in the jump; and William Wilson injured his back and had severe burns on the face and hands. Tom Robinson of Boston broke his leg jumping from a second-story window, and Joseph Beaupre of Mooers Forks suffered serious burns. The hotel manager's wife was forced to retreat into their room because of smoke and flames in the hallway outside their door. She jumped out the window, her night dress on fire, and suffered minor burns.

A coroner's inquest began on Saturday, two days after the tragedy. Although the cause of the fire was never definitively determined, it was believed to have originated in the partition between the barroom and the office, where the explosion seemed to occur. Owners William and Mary Wilson and manager W.M. Bailey were charged with manslaughter in the second degree for failing to provide proper fire escapes. Bailey was acquitted of culpability in February 1914. However, it took the jury several hours of deliberation before the jurors realized they would not be able to agree on the culpability of the Wilsons, so the case was discharged until the following year. Robideau, upon whose death the case was built, *could* have escaped with those he was alerting as he ran up and down the halls, but he returned to his room and there met his fate. Some of the jury believed that a fire escape, had there been one, would not have been able to save him at that point. Others felt that maybe it could have. The case against the Wilsons was repeatedly delayed with every term of court, due to illness of witnesses, illness of the defendants, an attorney no-show and so on. Finally, a week short of three years after the fire, the Wilsons were found not guilty. Regardless, the Wilsons and Bailey had allegedly been told by the inspector to install fire escapes, and they didn't. As a result, seven people were dead, and nobody accepted responsibility for it.

BRADLEY POWDER HOUSE EXPLOSION

WATERTOWN, 1915

It was a pleasant Saturday afternoon in the city of Watertown. Schoolchildren with spring fever were playing hopscotch in the streets or tag in their backyards. Women were pushing baby carriages along State Street and around Public Square while window-shopping. Little girls skipped alongside them, toting teddy bears or dolls, while their brothers stayed home playing with toy soldiers on the sidewalk or marbles in the gutter. Older boys, well, if they weren't working, they were likely to be riding their bikes or looking for an out-of-the-way spot for target practice to hone their hunting skills. It was just another ordinary Saturday. Until it wasn't.

Shortly after 1:00 p.m., the city shuddered so violently that some thought it was the end of the world. With a tremendous bang, countless windows shattered—including many large plate-glass panes in the business section—chimneys crumbled and plaster cracked. The jolt knocked some people to their knees, while others received cuts and abrasions from falling glass and debris. The *Ogdensburg Advance* of May 13, 1915, said:

> *State and Court streets seem to have suffered most of the business buildings. Every window in the Gray building in State Street was broken, and four of the largest were blown entirely in. In the section of the city between Washington and Franklin streets nearest the explosion, no house escaped, and in the majority of cases the glass was cleared from the sashes as though a knife had cut it.*

The *Commercial Advertiser* of May 11, 1915, added, "Much damage was done throughout the city, plate glass windows being broken in the very heart of the city and buildings shaken and damaged at many points, the houses on the street where the explosion occurred being all more or less wrecked." Dazed and shaken, city residents stumbled out into the streets, if they weren't already outside, in a growing chorus of concern and panic. *What just happened?* Soon they discovered that Thomas H. Bradley's Powder House between Gotham and Washington Streets on the outskirts of the city had exploded, when its contents were struck by the bullet of one of the two boys using the storage unit for target practice. Both boys—Earl J. Riordan, seventeen, and Almont J. Connolly, nineteen—died instantly, so nobody knows who made the kill shot or what their reason was for choosing that location. Was it a dare? Tempting fate? The invincible attitude so often attributed to teenagers? Was it ignorance of their surroundings and the potential results of their actions? Or was it just random, misguided happenstance? We will never know, because the two took the details to their graves, and there were no witnesses. All we know is that they were at ground zero and were blown to bits. The *Watertown Re-Union* of May 12, 1915, reported:

> *The nearest houses to the point where the explosion occurred are nearly half a mile away, and many of these were badly wrecked, the windows being blown out and the interiors shattered. The nearest house, that of E.H. Truesdell, had the plaster torn from the walls upstairs and down, the back door blown into the house and dishes and other breakable articles smashed. The home of James Pogue, next to that of Truesdell, is in a similar plight, as is the home of Percy Chinery, across the road....At the City Hospital, nearly a mile away, many windows were broken, especially in the operating room, where an operation had just been completed and the patient removed, and also in the sun parlor.*

The papers, in the blatant way they detailed gruesome events in those days, described what was found at the scene. The *Ogdensburg Advance* and *St. Lawrence Weekly Democrat* said the boys were apparently using the building in which explosives were stored as a target and described the scene in the immediate aftermath:

> *Six rods of stone fence were destroyed by the explosion. The building was of wood, eight feet long, five feet wide and eight feet high, and contained both powder and dynamite. Where the building stood is a large crater, in*

which there is not a shred of wood left, which would indicate that anything had been there. The building was painted red....A circular hole, over 30 feet across and five feet deep, blown to the solid rock and with a bottom as smooth as though a scraper had shaped it marked the site of the 12 by 15 foot building that is believed to have contained six tons of dynamite.... From 100 to 200 feet all about the hole, where a grassy pasture had been in the morning, the ground was ripped and torn like a plowed field and literally strewn with rocks. Overturned trees, broken limbs, and ripped up bushes marked the scene of the explosion for a thousand feet.

The article mentioned a theory floating around that one of the victims was standing near the building while the other was shooting at it. This conjecture surfaced because of where the bodies and two .22-caliber rifles were found.

Two boys target shooting. *Author's collection.*

In this scenario, Connelly may have placed a tin can on top of the magazine structure housing the dynamite and was standing somewhat near it when Riordan fired the fateful shot, which inadvertently penetrated the building and set off the large quantity of dynamite stored within. The *Ogdensburg Advance* and *St. Lawrence Weekly Democrat* added:

> *As the explosion occurred, Connely* [sic] *was blown in the direction of Gotham street and parts of his body were strewn all along for a distance of more than a thousand feet. That he was blown along the ground was shown by the window his body made through the dense bushes, and endless twigs were broken off in the path of the boy. There was not enough left of Connely for identification except his clothes and possibly his hair.*
>
> *Earl Riordan was about a hundred feet away from the accident and is thought to have been shooting from the stump of a fallen tree at this point. The tree probably served as a shield in some respects and prevented his body from being blown farther. Riordan was badly mutilated, his right leg being blown off, as also was his right arm. His clothes were entirely blown from his body, and his face was badly mutilated.*

One of the first officers at the scene was Officer Owen Hendricks, and he stood beside the remains of Riordan, "warning women away," because the "mass bore little resemblance to a human being," according to the *Advertiser*. The article said, "Riordan's body was an unrecognizable mass, disemboweled, with every bone in the body apparently broken." He had been wearing a blue suit. Bits of Connelly's body, which were discovered a while after Riordan's, were found in many places within one thousand feet of the explosion. The search for his body occurred only because first responders found pieces of brown coat (which Riordan was wearing) mixed in with pieces of the blue suit Connelly was wearing. The force of the explosion was so powerful that the bodies were blown into many pieces scattered helter-skelter; these were gathered up and placed in Guilfoyle's ambulance once it arrived to take the remains, such as they were, to the morgue.

The boys were best friends and popular high school students who had taken up hunting on weekends. On this day, they were engaged in target practice for either their next big hunt or because they were simply bored. Riordan was a Watertown native and the only child of Mr. and Mrs. Orlo Riordan of 300 South Pleasant Street. His mother went into shock and was under the care of a doctor who assigned her a constant bedside nurse. Connelly was born in Henderson but had lived at 1022 Boyd Street in Watertown for two years. His father, Captain John A. Connolly, was manning a ship on the Great Lakes and could not be notified until he reached Chicago, where he was told by telegram that his son had died—he was not told how until he made it back to Watertown. By then, some fifteen thousand people from the surrounding area had visited the scene of the accident. The *Watertown Re-Union* of May 12, 1915, said as many as five hundred automobiles stopped by to view the enormous crater left by the explosion the day after it occurred, and "three distinct paths were worn by the pedestrians through the cow pasture leading to the powder house ruins."

Because the boys were well-liked high school students, many classmates showed up at the funerals over the next several days. Riordan's funeral was held at the family home on Pleasant Street on Tuesday with the Reverend Duane Johnson of the Asbury Methodist Episcopal Church officiating. He was buried at the North Watertown cemetery with several of his friends acting as pallbearers. On Wednesday, Connelly's funeral was also held at his home, as was customary at the time. The Reverend Darwin Pickard of the First Presbyterian Church officiated, and burial was at Roberts Corners.

Coroner H.L. Smith ordered an inquest to be held at once. Not only did he hope to find out what exactly happened but also whether the powder house was built to code and was lawfully located in a safe zone at the time of the incident. The *Ogdensburg Journal* of May 10, 1915, said:

> *A city ordinance prohibits the storing of explosives within the city. Mr. Bradley said the building was erected according to specifications of the State Fire Marshal's office and approved. Specifications, he said, require that the building be covered with bullet-proof iron or metal and that there be a wall of crushed stone or gravel. An inspection of the building was made this year.*

At the opening session of the inquest, the *Watertown Herald* reported that Bradley's attorney, John H. O'Brien, proved that "verbal permission had been granted to Thomas Bradley to place his powder house on the site within the city limits where it was located when it was blown up." Although many structures in the city sustained a substantial amount of damage from the explosion, the inquest showed that Thomas Bradley could not be held liable for the damage, nor could the City of Watertown. It was determined that the explosion was caused by a gunshot into the powder house; however, they would never know which boy fired the shot and therefore could not place blame or liability on either victim's family.

DEADLY CHRISTMAS EVE MUNITIONS PLANT EXPLOSION

WATERTOWN, 1918

It was the afternoon of Christmas Eve 1918 in Watertown, and the mood on the streets and in most homes was appropriately merry. Storefront windows were brightly decorated to celebrate the season. Children were giddy with expectation, perhaps hoping for a jack-in-the-box or a floppy Raggedy Ann doll. Come evening, there would be holiday music programs to attend, Christmas trees to light, mistletoe under which to kiss, brandy-soaked raisins and chestnuts to roast, ghost stories like *A Christmas Carol* to read and carols to sing. Stockings would be hung on the mantel, and cookies and milk would be left on the table for jolly old Saint Nicholas. The magic of Christmas was alive and well in Northern New York. But it was Wednesday, midafternoon, and many people still had to get through the remainder of their workday before participating in the traditional Christmas Eve activities. Unfortunately, seven Watertown employees (five women and two men) would never make it home to join their families in the festivities, and the merry mood in the city would become one of mourning as word spread of another horrific tragedy.

At 2:50 p.m., a primer cap detonated at the J.B. Wise loading department building on Water Street, setting off a series of deadly explosions within the small, one-hundred-by-fifty-foot frame structure. There was no warning, and those standing closest to ground zero never stood a chance of escaping. While the main portion of the plant was barely damaged, the loading department toppled "like a house of cards" in the explosions and resultant inferno, according to various reports. As was the case three years earlier with

Waiting for Santa, circa 1918. *Author's collection.*

the explosion of the Bradley Powder House, residents far and wide heard and felt the blast. For a moment, Watertown citizens stopped in their tracks and looked around in puzzlement, wondering what was happening. Soon the gruesome details of the explosion would become known, as they always do, and there would be tales of lucky survivors, as well as kind words for the deceased, as there always are. It seems that in nearly every disaster, we hear tales of those on whom Lady Luck cast her fair hand—and those on whom she did not. That day, she looked favorably upon John Burns, the outdoor guard on duty at the plant.

Burns said he was inside the sentry shack, which was only a few feet away from the loading building, when he heard the explosion and was knocked to the ground. After debris stopped pummeling the guard shack roof, he hurried out and turned back to see his shelter reduced to kindling and the loading building engulfed. He knew his coworkers were in peril, so he rushed directly into the danger to assist, grateful that his life had been spared. So, too, was the life of a baby boy in the Clark residence at nearby 801 Water Street. The infant was asleep in his crib when an entire window (frame and glass) was blown directly down on him, according to the *Ogdensburg Republican-Journal* of December 26, 1918. Although badly shaken, he miraculously escaped injury. One woman, Mamie Corbine, who lived just down the street from the Wise loading dock, was taking a nap when her bedroom window blew in, and she was thrown from her bed across the floor, sustaining bruises and an injured arm. She was among the fortunate. The same article said, "Not a pane of glass in the Clark or Corine house, or any others in the neighborhood, were left intact. Limbs were blown from trees…porches were wrecked."

Louise Portt saw it all coming. The forty-year-old woman was a government inspector at the Wise plant by day and a fortune-teller by night, according to an article by Dave Shampine in the *Watertown Daily Times* on March 11, 2001. Portt worked at the Wise plant and had read the cards for her coworker Jennie Raymond the day before the disaster. The article said the cards drawn were all spades. Not good. Spades is the suit of negativity—of setbacks, losses, death and so on. Portt told Raymond that something terrible would happen to Jennie and to someone beside her the next day. The "someone beside her" turned out to be Louise Portt herself. She was standing next to Raymond near the back door when the simultaneous blasts rang out.

Eldese E. Larabee was foreman on duty in the loading building that day. In testimony, his superintendent, Milton Neff, called him a man of

Brothers William Edward and John Wesley Black. *Courtesy of their great-nephew, Thomas F. LaClair, town of Clayton historian.*

good character and habits, saying that, indeed, he was so well liked by his subordinates that they had given him a Christmas gift just hours before the explosion that killed him. Larabee had been working for Wise for seven months. On December 24, he had his work cut out for him because the loading department's regular mechanic was off that day, so the job of making minor repairs to machinery fell to Larabee and eighteen-year-old Wesley Black. That afternoon, only one of the six loading machines was working reliably, so a great deal of time was being wasted trying to get the others up and running. Understandably, this would be frustrating to the foreman in charge of twenty-five employees looking to him for work assignments.

In her bedside interview for the inquest, according to the *Watertown Daily Times* of December 30, 1918, Portt recalled walking into the loading room for a moment, just before the explosion. At that time, Larabee, Wesley and William Black (brothers), as well as a "little French boy," were gathered around a machine they were trying to fix. The testimony said:

As she came back she saw that Larrabee [sic] was working with a hammer and long punch at the machine, endeavoring, as she expressed it, to make

the wheel go around. Witness testified to the effect that a primer was bent
and that Larrabee was pounding at it with the hammer and punch, which
she described as "a long piece of iron about as large around as her finger."

Portt also said she heard Larabee swear once (others said he never lost his temper) and that when she saw him pounding on the fuse, she felt he was being careless. Timothy McCarthy, a chief army inspector on site, also testified to seeing the men working on a jammed machine. McCarthy said it was generally understood that pincers were to be used to safely remove shells stuck in the machines, but "he had heard of Larabee using tools other than pincers to remove such shells." Testimony was given regarding the material the hammer and punch were made of because iron on iron and steel on steel could cause the spark that set off the primer powder. Survivors were also asked about safety exits (with some claiming they thought the doors were locked), smoking on the premises and housekeeping. (In other words, were the floors mopped sufficiently to not have loose powder accumulating underfoot?) In his final ruling as the city coroner, since his position had already been scheduled to be eliminated the following week, R.F. Gates of Brownville ruled simply that a primer at the plant became jammed into the roller, and when Larabee attempted to force it out, it exploded, killing seven and injuring nineteen. Two minutes after the explosion, a fire alarm sounded, alerting all available firemen and policemen to report to the scene and begin the gruesome task of rescue and recovery.

The dead included the four men surrounding the jammed machine: foreman Eldese E. Larabee, thirty-two, of 250 Arsenal Street and formerly of Norwood; Alfred Marculier, the sixteen-year-old French boy Mrs. Portt had spoken of, who lived at 111 East Moulton Street at the time; and brothers Wesley and William Black, eighteen and twenty years old, respectively, of 413 Meade Street. The *Ogdensburg Republican-Journal* of December 25, 1918, said:

The bodies of E.E. Larrabee and one of the Black brothers were recovered
from the ruins of the plant almost unrecognizable. Alfred Marculler [sic]
and the other of the Blacks were alive when dragged from the burning
building but died in a vacant house in Water street which was used as a
first-aid station.

Mrs. Louise Port [sic], wife of Edward Port, was missing for some
time after the accident and the police were fearful that her body would be

found in the ruins. It developed later, however, that she had escaped with serious burns and reached her home in the Burdick block by taxicab. Her condition was said there to be serious, but not critical.

The Marculier boy was identified by his father by the shoes and socks on his feet. Like Larabee and Black, his body and face were burned beyond recognition. Also killed were Ruby Abby, twenty-three, a young mother of a toddler who would spend Christmas without her momma. Abby lived at 883 Ann Street and was operating the only working machine that day. Rita Kirkpatrick, eighteen, of Fowler, who was feeding the machine, died next to her. Ruby Abby's mother, Nettie Shawcross, forty-five, was working near the two young women but somehow survived the blast. The *Ogdensburg Republican-Journal* reported, "Mrs. Abby, who was unconscious when carried out of the plant, died at St. Joachim's Hospital last night, and Miss Kirkpatrick died at the City Hospital at 8:30 o'clock." The Reverend Frank C. Marshall of Black River, age sixty-two, was also pulled from the rubble alive but soon died at the hospital. He had been a Baptist minister before being hired as a janitor at the Wise plant earlier that year. The *Courier & Freeman* of January 1, 1919, described the passing of Marshall:

It was with intense sorrow that the people of Nicholville learned of the tragic death of Rev. F.C. Marshall, a former Baptist pastor. His death on Friday resulted from burns received the Tuesday previous in an explosion which wrecked the munition plant at Watertown where he had been employed since last summer. He was severely burned, and his clothing tattered and practically destroyed by the flames. At once he was moved to St. Joachim's Hospital where he passed away....A few years ago he became afflicted with throat trouble which affected his voice and made preaching impossible and forcing his retirement from the ministry.

The Black family suffered three tragedies in one week's time. First, the handsome young brothers, William Edward and John Wesley, died horrifically in the Wise plant explosion. The official cause of death listed on John's death certificate was "burns of the face, body, and limbs, resulting from explosion." He had just celebrated his eighteenth birthday six days before he died. Twenty-year-old William's official cause of death was likewise listed as "burns of the face, body, and limbs, following explosion." Their father, Charles Edward Black, was in Oneida on business at the time of the tragedy, and the family was unable to reach him with the terrible news. He learned

John Wesley Black, certificate of death. *Courtesy of his great-nephew, Thomas F. LaClair, town of Clayton historian.*

of his only sons' deaths the way the rest of the North Country did—in a newspaper he picked up at the newsstand that evening. He hurried back to Watertown "prostrated with grief" and found that his wife had been placed under the care of a physician due to emotional shock. Then, exactly one week later, the boys' sister Maude (one of five daughters) died of diphtheria. The *Watertown Daily Times* of March 5, 1919, said:

> *Deputy Compensation Commissioner W. C. Richards made an award in Syracuse Tuesday of $23.46 a week to Mrs. Catherine Black of this city for the death of her two sons, Wesley Black, aged 18, and William Black,*

aged 20, who were killed in the explosion....According to the evidence submitted to the commissioner, the two men were the main support of their mother [and sisters] *at the time of the accident.*

Of the twenty-five workers in the loading building that day, not one escaped without some type of injury or death, according to most news accounts. The *Courier & Freeman* of New Year's Day 1919 described the injured as:

Miss Tillie Quinn aged about 40, right leg fractured below knee; Miss Helen Murray, severe scalp wounds; Miss Gertrude Fitzgibbons, aged about 43, all of Watertown, badly burned....Miss Bertha Irvine, aged 38, of Dexter, fingers of one hand so badly burned that amputation was necessary; Mrs. Ada Emberton, aged 33 of Watertown, both hands badly burned; Miss Carla Brownell, aged 18, of Brownville, hands burned and forehead contused; Miss Lena Stolzle, aged 19, Watertown, bruised about hips and face; Mrs. Luke Salisbury, aged 30, Black River road, badly bruised; Mrs. Nettie Shawcross, Watertown, badly bruised; Mrs. Louise Portt, Watertown, severe burns; Mrs. Jennie Raymond, Watertown, aged about 45, was blown through the door of the building as it was forced from its hinges.

John Burns, the outdoor plant guard mentioned previously, provided the following statement regarding what he had witnessed to the *Courier & Freeman* on January 1:

"I was inside the sentry box when the explosion happened," said Capt. Burns. "There was but one explosion and it made a terrific noise and flames and sheets of fire seemed to leap from all parts of the building. Every window in the guard house was broken, and the timbers and the wreckage seemed to rain on the roof, some of the heavy girders breaking through, but I was uninjured.

"I have worked enough in blasting to stay under cover until the wreckage stops falling, but when the timbers had stopped coming down, I ran outside and around thro' the adjoining building to the loading room. As I crawled in through a window, it was certainly a horrible sight. Girls were trying to crawl out from under the wreckage and their screams could be heard for blocks.

"I saw the Kirkpatrick girl laid out on the floor under some heavy timbers and girders. She was conscious and begged me to release her. 'For God's

sake, get me out from under this,' she begged. I tried to move the girders, but they were so heavy that it would take half a dozen men to move them.

"Men came running from the shops and the work of getting the bodies out was soon under way. As I ran out of the sentry box, I saw two girls crawling out on the ground, but I did not stop, for I wanted to get inside the wrecked building. Wreckage was strewn all over the neighborhood and made the rescue work more difficult."

Another employee, Harry Ross, who was in the room adjoining the one where the explosion took place, offered this firsthand account to the paper:

I saw the whole thing through a window. The walls seemed to crumple up just like paper. The roof went to pieces as tho' someone had crushed it between his hands. I jumped through a window and discovered Larrabee face downward on the floor near the front wall. I picked him up and carried him outside and then went back and carried out a girl who was bleeding and unconscious. The wreckage was everywhere and fell like hailstones all around us.

In the next room to the loading plant, there were 100 boxes of the primer caps but they were not exploded. If the force of the explosion had come toward us in that room, instead of toward the main plant, the whole plant would probably have been blown up and many more lives lost. As it was, I can't see how so many of the girls escaped with their lives, for they had no warning.

Even amid multiple funerals for his employees, tighter scrutiny of operations, public outrage and a grueling two-day inquest, C. Ralph Wise kept his factory open, working his employees harder than ever. Two weeks after the Christmas Eve tragedy, however, many employees walked off the job and went on strike when told they would begin working ten-hour days without overtime pay, according to Shampine's 2001 article in the *Watertown Daily Times*. And just two months after the explosion that killed so many people working for him, thirty-six-year-old owner C. Ralph Wise died of pneumonia on February 26, 2019. Wise's infamous Water Street facility was shuttered that May.

EXPLODING SHELL KILLS EIGHT CHILDREN

WATERTOWN, 1922

It seemed to keep happening every three or so years. The city of Watertown was rocked by yet another explosion in the summer of 1922. This time, it was not the result of a dynamite magazine being used for target practice. It was not the result of a primer cap for war ammunition detonating after getting jammed in a roller. No, this time it was the result of a perfect storm—the combination of a "dud" shell taken from the Pine Plains (Fort Drum) reservation as a souvenir and left on the back porch of an apartment house; eight children engaged in an innocent game of croquet in the backyard of that same house; and a ninety-six-degree day, so hot that it could cause TNT in a dud to expand and explode at the slightest touch. There were nearly as many theories as there were victims. Did a child unwittingly set it off? It had sat in the same open, exposed spot and had been handled often for a year. Was it accidently bumped and knocked over? Or was it a ticking time bomb pushed over the top by the high temperature? The exact reason the dud exploded was never ascertained with absolute certainty. But one thing is undebatable—the blast was responsible for the death of eight children. And none of them ever knew what hit them.

The so-called dud was a six-inch-wide, two-foot-tall, one-hundred-pound artillery shell found in a field at Pine Plains (now Fort Drum) the year before and brought home as a souvenir by Edward G. Workman to use as a lamp base or a conversation starter, the latter of which it would certainly become, in an unanticipated manner. Workman and his family lived on the first floor of a duplex at 423 Dimmick Street, while the second floor was occupied by the William L. Salisbury family. At the time of the tragedy, the dud was being used as a doorstop on the back porch. Obviously, it was believed inoperative and harmless to the constant traffic of youngsters at play. The *Courier and Freeman* of July 19, 1922, provided the following details known about the deadly object:

> *The shell was what is commonly known as a "dud," the projectile which had been fired from one of the six-inch howitzers during the target practice of the One Hundred and Sixth heavy field artillery at the reservation last summer, but which had not exploded by fuse or contact, and lay in the sand fully charged....*
>
> *The shell is one left at the Plains about six years ago, according to information given by the war department, which showed that that type of shell had not been used at the Plains since 1916. The shell had been in the possession of Mr. Workman for the last two years and during that time had undergone some severe usage, having been hammered often....*

At 2:55 p.m. on that sweltering, sunny Wednesday afternoon, the children of the household, along with several friends from the neighborhood, were engaged in a game of croquet in the backyard when one of them, sixteen-year-old Morris Salisbury, who lived upstairs and was an only child, was seen climbing the steps of the back porch, where the dud acted as a door jam. A neighbor, Mrs. William J. Semper, was watching the children play from her kitchen window when she saw the boy, and she told investigators he had nothing in his hands at that time. The last thing she saw him do was wipe his hair off his face with both hands, and then there was an explosion. She "looked out but could see nothing but a cloud of black smoke and dust rising skyward," according to the paper. The house, made of heavy concrete blocks, was completely blown out at the rear and its wooden roof blown clear off. The windows in houses within two blocks of the blast were shattered. But as the dust settled and frantic family members, neighbors and rescuers rushed to the scene, they realized the situation was far worse than just structural damage. The children were gone. One moment they were laughing and playing and full of life, the next they were instantly hurled into heaven, leaving their mangled, mortal, youthful bodies behind.

The blast was so powerful that pieces of clothing were found in neighbors' yards, on tree branches and on fences in the vicinity. One woman who lived a quarter mile away was standing outside and was struck so hard by a stone from the blast that it broke her hand. Attorney Charles A. Phelps

Young girls playing croquet, circa 1922. *Author's collection.*

was the first to arrive at the scene and saw the explosion as he was driving down Ten Eyck Street. He told the *Ogdensburg Republican-Journal* of July 13, 1922, that the building "surged outward and upward with a force that indicated that there was stored there either a large amount of dynamite or a very high-powered shell."

Dr. E.W. Jones was one of the first doctors on the scene. He was horrified to discover that one of the dead was his very own daughter Vivian. He knew from the bandage he had just placed on her leg that morning. Somehow, he stifled his horror and grief, covered her body back up carefully and continued searching for those who might still be alive and in need of immediate attention. Unfortunately, none of the children playing in the Workman yard that day were still alive. He later learned that his younger daughter, Mabel, nearly met the same fate as the others. The *Courier and Freeman* said:

> *Pretty little 7-year-old Mabel Jones, sister of Vivian Jones, one of the victims, and daughter of Dr. and Mrs. E.W. Jones, hardly realizing the great calamity which befell her sister* [was] *told Thursday of her escape from being one of the victims also. Mabel is the only one of the children who played in the Workman yard that afternoon that was not killed.*
>
> *"When they started to play croquet they told me I was too small," she said woefully. "They told me I had better go home and so I did." There she sought solace of her mother, who told her that possibly she could play with the others later.*

Of course, later would never come for the others. Seven of the eight children died instantly, and their blackened bodies were mangled almost beyond recognition, some missing limbs or heads. But what little clothing remained intact helped in identification. Their bodies were all found "within a semi-circular arch from 25 to 30 feet from the porch," as if they had been

A sad young boy and girl, circa 1922. *Author's collection.*

in a huddle awaiting their turns in their game, and when the blast occurred, their bodies were evenly dispersed in equal distances. Their mallets and balls lay beside them, suggesting that they'd been holding them at the moment of impact. Morris Salisbury's body was found buried beneath concrete blocks that had been blown off the house and porch in the blast. Some pieces of block were found twenty-five feet away. He was alive when the ambulance got there but died within five minutes of reaching the city hospital.

At sixteen, Morris had been the oldest of the victims. He was well liked and admired for his musical ability playing the violin. The other victims were Frances Wylie, the thirteen-year-old daughter of Fannie Wylie of 328 Ten Eyck Street; Vivian Jones, twelve-year-old daughter of Dr. and Mrs. E.W. Jones of 341 Mullin Street; Olin Brown, eleven-year-old son of Mr. and Mrs. George A. Brown of 410 Dimmick Street; Anson Workman, thirteen-year-old son of the Workmans, and his sister, Edna, who was fourteen years old; Sarah Barden, thirteen-year-old daughter of Mr. and Mrs. E.W. Bardon of 415 Dimmick Street; and Donald Horton, twelve-year-old son of Mr. and Mrs. A.D. Horton of Pulaski. He was visiting Olin Brown. Mr. and Mrs. Workman were away at the time of the explosion. One can only imagine the depth of their grief, learning their children died in such a horrific manner from an item brought home as a souvenir.

Mr. and Mrs. Salisbury were both home in the front of their upstairs apartment, along with their mothers, Mary Salisbury and Margaret Munro. While the children played outside, Mr. Salisbury had tried to convince his mother to go out back in the yard where the children were playing and sit under the tree, as it would be cooler than staying indoors, but she wanted to stay inside. And his mother-in-law had just returned inside after cooling off in the yard when the explosion occurred. The lives of all four adults were spared, but their only child, the grandson their mothers had come to visit, lost his young life.

The *Sandy Creek News* of July 13, 1922, described the ensuing investigation:

> *Captain G.H. Schumaker, construction quartermaster temporarily at Madison Barracks, First artillery expert, inspected the ruins of the porch and pieces of the projectile with other army officers, and materially aided District Attorney E. Robert Wilcox, coroner of Jefferson County, in determining facts concerning the shell and its effects.*
>
> *Captain Schumaker stated that the excessive heat, causing T.N.T. charge to expand, would materially increase the possibility of explosion, although not of itself causing the shell to blow up. Under such conditions, a jar of*

much less intensity than otherwise needed, might explode the shell, he said. Captain Schumaker said that there is no safe way to unload a "dud" shell, save at an arsenal, where they are exploded through the aid of bombproofs [sic]. *He advised throwing them in the river.*

Captain Schumaker also stated that in warfare, anyone within one hundred yards of detonation of such a shell would be killed, and pieces of metal, stone or other material could be hurled at least a half mile away, as in the case of the woman who was struck on the hand by a piece of debris from the Workman explosion.

The joint funeral for all the children was held at the Arsenal Street Sanctuary Chapel two days later. Mr. and Mrs. Workman remained living in their home, following its repairs, until he died in 1953, and she died a year after him in a nursing home. Mrs. Salisbury remained in her upstairs apartment at 423 Dimmick until the house was sold. The house remains today, looking much the same as it did on the day of that horrible disaster so long ago.

AU SABLE FORKS IS PREY TO FLAMES

AU SABLE FORKS, 1925

On Wednesday morning, May 13, 1925, an electrical wiring expert for the New York State Underwriters paid a visit to the Forks, as Au Sable Forks is dubbed. He met with the town's electrician to see if a recently designated hazardous situation had been addressed yet, because substantially higher insurance rates had to be paid by the property owners for such hazardous findings until the problems were remedied. The wiring in the basement of the "Smith block" was defective. Wires were pressed snugly against boards intended to protect them, but there was supposed to be at least a two-inch gap between the wall boards and the wires. The town's electrician, according to the *Plattsburgh Sentinel* on May 19, 1925, promised the state's wiring expert that he would take care of it soon, but he was busy and couldn't do it then. The next morning, a fire began in the basement of Candyland in the Smith block, resulting in the death of a firefighter and the devastation of an entire community.

F.J. Bonville, manager of the *Ausable Forks Record-Post*, was not about to get "scooped" on a story that happened in his own backyard. His weekly paper was prepared for publication every Wednesday evening and published for Thursday morning release. When the "biggest story in his newspaper life" was staring him straight in the face, he became determined to break the news first and to do so as accurately as possible. Power outage, regular workplace, usual story-writing tools and deadlines be damned; he would overcome every obstacle, and there were many that terrible night, to alert the affected community and all of the Forks' neighboring communities to

Main Street, Au Sable Forks, circa 1920. *Author's collection.*

the disaster that had befallen his beloved town that day. He laid it all out in as thorough and methodical detail as he possibly could at that relatively early juncture. The following details are based off his and others' reporting.

The fire started in the H. Smith & Company building early the morning of May 14, just a few minutes past one o'clock. It was discovered by James Hodges, who lived with his wife over Candyland, when he was awakened to the unmistakable smell of smoke in his room. At that point, he could already see strands of smoke in their room, so he threw on some clothes, told his wife what was happening and ran out to sound the alarm. The earliest first responders realized that the Smith building, with Candyland in its basement, was already lost, when they saw heavy smoke pouring over the roof of the four-story building Hodges lived and worked in. A fire whistle summoned the firefighters of the community to the scene, and the hydrant on Main Street was tapped into with a line of hose to attempt to stem the flames. But a stiff breeze was blowing early that morning, and the fire leapt unbridled from store to store and house to house, content with an abundance of old wooden structures to feast on. More help was definitely needed. Other fire departments were called in, and every one of them responded as quickly as possible: Plattsburgh, Lake Placid, Saranac Lake, Willsborough and others.

Au Sable Forks spans two counties—Essex and Clinton—and the Au Sable River acts as the boundary separating the counties. That fateful day, the business section on the Essex County side of the river was the primary target. According to the "Extra Fire Edition" of the *Adirondack Record-Elizabethtown Post* of May 14, 1925, the fire swiftly destroyed the Smith building and the town of Jay supervisor Fred Terrance's adjoining old bank building. Becoming more and more powerful and swift with each building it consumed, the fire continued its path of ruin, taking down the home of Dr. L.J.L. Avery and an adjoining apartment building, the residence of Alice Trumbell, the Methodist Episcopal Church, the Stearns residence and, finally (in the southerly direction), the Knights of Columbus hall, where it was halted. Sweeping in a northerly direction, the fire took the Au Sable House and the Au Sable Auto Supply Company before pausing at the M.&A. Meconi fruit store, which was a concrete structure. No amount of the fire's huffing and puffing could blow the concrete in. But it did break and melt the glass windows of the fruit store and the dental office overhead.

Now more voracious than ever, the fire leapt across the street to the east side, wreaking havoc on the Fitzsimmons residence, Dennis Longtemps's home, the Meigs duplex and Hollis Jacques's home. It gutted the beautiful, old Episcopal church and another duplex owned by the Rogers Company. Setting their sights on the Bosley Block, the flames feasted on several doctors' offices, the Foresters' hall, an electric shop, a plumbing shop, a pharmacy and a poolroom. The Featherston block lost an apartment building; the Au Sable Vulcanizing Company block lost its office and salesroom, a barbershop, a North Country museum, a tailor's shop and a room occupied by the Keeseville Telephone Company exchange. After several more homes and apartment buildings had been consumed, along with a variety store, a bar and a photo studio, the fire reached its final destination—the Au Sable Supply Company's general store—thanks to the valiant efforts of the Plattsburgh Fire Department, whose volunteers were concentrating their efforts on that building. It was here, at the last stop, that the greatest tragedy of the entire disaster would occur.

Two or three firefighters were battling the flames from the roof of the general store, until they realized it was time to find their way down. Once on the ground, Fireman Charles Riley collapsed from smoke inhalation and had to be carried to doctors at the American House on the other side of the river. Meanwhile, George Lefebvre entered from the rear of the structure, unaware that the others had all left the building because it had become too unsafe to stay inside or on the roof. The *Record-Post* stated that Lefebvre was then "trapped in a seething furnace but groped his way through the blinding smoke while the flames licked his body." Those still working on spraying down the front of the building were not aware anyone was still inside, until

Firemen at work. *Library of Congress, Prints and Photographs Division.*

Lefebvre staggered through the front door, having made his way through the burning building, and collapsed in the arms of his Plattsburgh comrades. Lefebvre was carried across the river to the American House, where a priest gave the fireman last rites while waiting for an ambulance to arrive from the Champlain Valley hospital in Plattsburgh.

The *Plattsburgh Sentinel* of May 19, 1925, announced Lefebvre's death in an article titled, "Plattsburgh Hero Fireman Loses Fight." For more than four decades, George and his brother Fred had been fighting fires. They were endearingly dubbed "smoke eaters," because they never missed a call "to battle with the flames." They loved the job of firefighting. But on that night, in that building, the fifty-six-year-old George had literally swallowed flames, and thereafter, until his final breath, "every breath meant agony," according to the article. Yet the courageous man did not complain of his injuries. He knew family members gathered around his bedside were afraid to speak because they didn't want him to suffer by trying to respond. Nevertheless, he replied with great compassion to their silence. The looks of concern and the emotional struggles they were all feeling prompted him to reassure them in their time of need, as he whispered again and again, "I'm all right." At 9:23 p.m., the fireman's unspeakable suffering ended. Left to grieve and carry on were his widow, Sophie; his daughter, May; and his son, Victor—as well as three brothers, four sisters and his Plattsburgh Fire Department family.

Initially, forty-five families were reported to have lost their homes and all their possessions. However, that number climbed to fifty-seven families who had been left destitute and in need of assistance. Many had left their homes with only the clothes on their backs. The Au Sable Forks Relief Fund was quickly established to raise $50,000 for relief of the affected families. Ten thousand letters were mailed out to regional churches, service organizations and people. To kick things off, the American Red Cross donated $1,000 and sent a Red Cross employee and accountant from Tupper Lake to assist, so the Au Sable Forks residents could concentrate on other things. The relief fund monies would go toward furnishings, clothing, new homes, and food, as needed. The Red Cross assumed all administrative fees, so every penny donated would go directly to those in need. Generous donations poured in from every direction, in the form of dollars, truckloads of food and clothing collected from other communities, and manual assistance of many types. When the needs of individuals were well on their way to having been met, attention was given to rebuilding the business section. As is often the case, the devastating fire proved to be the impetus for Au Sable Forks to rebuild. The residents used the opportunity, however tragically it arrived, to modernize and beautify their business section, and to make their homes and businesses safer than before.

TENEMENT FIRE CLAIMS SEVEN LIVES

SARANAC LAKE, 1925

A great tragedy unfolded at the Murphy apartments in the heart of Saranac Lake's business district early the morning of Independence Day 1925. The wooden structure at 105 Broadway, which had formerly been operated as the Adirondack House hotel, was considered a three-story tinderbox—a disaster waiting to happen. It is believed that the 4:00 a.m. fire, which was of unknown origin, began at the rear of the first floor and quickly blocked the stairs, which were the only form of access to and egress from the second and third floors. The entire building became so quickly engulfed that firefighters were unable to enter for two hours after arriving on scene and spraying with every available hose. The central fire station was only one hundred feet away, and it had taken the firefighters only moments to assemble and rush to the fire, according to the *Adirondack Record-Elizabethtown Post* of July 9, 1925. But the fire was too fast and fierce, the wood of the structure too dry and old, and it was already too late to save anyone who had not gotten out in those harrowing first several moments. To their great credit, however, the firemen, under the direction of Chief E.W. Harrison, were able to prevent the fire from spreading to nearby structures in the crowded district.

The night before, the nineteen occupants had gone to bed thinking about the fireworks and festivities of the next day. Only twelve lived to see the next day come. It was estimated that one in ten similar tenements in Saranac Lake at that time offered no fire escapes or reliable means of egress from fire, which was a violation of village ordinances, but there was nobody who enforced those regulations, so there was plenty of blame to go around for

Flames surround structure. *Author's collection, iStock image.*

such a tragedy. The owner of the building was John Murphy of St. Regis Falls, who, with his wife, kept rooms on the second floor when they were in town, according to the *Adirondack News*. (Other articles, however, stated that the couple lived next door.) Murphy had just returned from a serious operation in Plattsburgh the day before the tragedy, and, although he was technically in charge of the building, he would have been in no condition to help when disaster struck.

The individual stories of the seven who died are horribly dismal. For example, sixteen-year-old Robert McGowan and his brother, twenty-one-year-old Joseph McGowan, fell asleep thinking about making something of themselves in the quaint Adirondack village, but their dreams were snuffed out when they died of smoke inhalation in their sleep. They had arrived in Saranac Lake that very evening with barely more than the clothes on their backs and were unable to find an affordable place to sleep until sixty-five-year-old Patrick Martin of Chateaugay kindly offered to share his room at the Murphy place with them until they could find work. Once it was safe enough to enter the structure, Chief of Police Frank E. Sheldon found the bodies of all three. Robert, who had been a student at Mount Assumption Institute in Plattsburgh the prior year, was lying on a mattress on the floor; his older brother, Joseph, was lying on the bed with his head "pillowed on his right arm," as if he was simply sleeping comfortably, according to the *Chateaugay Record* of July 10, 1925. After an exhausting day of travel and walking, the boys were likely asleep as soon as their heads hit their pillows. And just like that, they were gone. The bodies of the brothers were picked up by family members and taken back to their home in Burlington.

Old Man Martin's body was found slumped over a windowsill, burned beyond recognition. It appeared that he had attempted to escape or call for help out the window but was overcome and collapsed in the process. Peter Dwyer of Saranac Lake was fifty-five years old. He was found dead in his bed, and it is believed that he was so tired after returning from work at midnight that he fell into a deep sleep and didn't hear the commotion before he succumbed to smoke inhalation. Because Dwyer and Martin had no known family, there was a double funeral for them on July 7, 1925, at St. Bernard's Roman Catholic Church. The streets of the entire village were respectfully silent, according to the *Plattsburgh Sentinel*, during the funeral hours of these and the other victims buried that day.

The Moniky family was sleeping on the second floor when they were awakened by the commotion. Finding that their way down the staircase was blocked by fire and their room had quickly filled with smoke, Charles Moniky headed to the window, telling his wife, Sarah, and their eleven-year-old son, Kenneth, that he would jump first and catch them. While the jump only slightly injured Charles, Sarah suffered minor injuries when her jump knocked them both down and she was cut climbing out of the window. Charles shot to his feet to catch his son, but the young boy stood in the window, too petrified to jump after seeing both parents have such a hard landing. Then he stepped away from view, apparently hoping to find a different way out, and his fate was sealed. His charred body was found in the hallway next to another victim. Sarah Moniky, whose emotional wounds were far greater to bear than anything she physically sustained, was taken to the Saranac General Hospital and recovered. The body of their son, Kenneth, was shipped to his mother's former home in Bangor for burial.

The remaining victims of the fire were George Duckett, twenty-one, and his infant son of Saranac Lake. Duckett, his young wife and their baby boy were tenants on the third floor. As firemen approached and began hosing down the structure so they could get in, they saw Mrs. Duckett appear in the window, yelling, "Catch my baby!" Once she saw that they had caught her precious bundle, she leaped herself, at the behest of her husband, who insisted his family was safely out of harm's way before jumping through the blazing curtains himself. To the horror of the firemen who caught the bundle, they discovered that it was only a pillow. In her terror and haste, and in the fogginess of mind one might experience when so abruptly awakened, she believed she was tossing her *child* to safety. Hours later, when the fire was finally extinguished, the tiny charred remains of Baby Boy Duckett were discovered in his cradle. Meanwhile, the young couple lay crumpled on the ground, nearly lifeless and unaware of the terrible mistake. They were scooped up and rushed to the Saranac General Hospital with terrible burns and multiple severe injuries after the jump. George Duckett died shortly after arriving at the hospital, and services for he and his son were held at St. Bernard's Roman Catholic Church the same day as Dwyer and Martin's funeral.

Duckett's wife was in too critical of condition to attend the services. For six weeks, she remained hospitalized in Saranac Lake, and many times it was believed that she might join her husband and son on the other side. Instead, she lived to tell about it. Indeed, the inquest into the tragedy was delayed several times until Mrs. Duckett, whom coroner John A. Farrell and district attorney Harold W. Main believed was a key witness with important testimony, was well enough to discuss the matter. And Dr. Edward S. Wells, whom they had questioned about Mrs. Duckett's condition, informed them that he expected she would pull through. So, on July 9, the investigation was "indefinitely adjourned." Mrs. Duckett was released from the hospital the third week of August 1925. But in mid-November, she was taken to a hospital in Rochester, New York, for treatment of her right arm and shoulder, which had become paralyzed from her injuries. An operation was her only hope to regain use of her arm.

Meanwhile, the people of Saranac Lake took it upon themselves to do something about a situation destined to repeat itself if actions were not taken to better protect themselves and their village from deadly fires. They demanded that proper exits and fire escapes be added to certain types of properties, as required by law. Chief of Police Sheldon was appointed as special fire inspector, according to the *Lake Placid News* of July 17, 1925, and he began inspecting apartment buildings and tenements at once. Many property owners were expected to be found in violation. But it was at least a start. While the value of lost property was estimated to be at $50,000 ($750,000 today), the value of the loss of life was incalculable.

THIRTY DIE IN SINKING
OF THE *JOHN B. KING*

MORRISTOWN AND BROCKVILLE, 1930

The thunderstorms of June 26, 1930, were considered "of only moderate energy" by meteorologists at the Canton weather bureau, but a single bolt of lightning just before the dinner hour made that date one of the most infamous in Northern New York and eastern Ontario maritime history when it struck tons of dynamite on a doomed drilling boat. The violent explosion hurled thirty-one men into the stormy sky, into the cold water and into the afterlife.

The *John B. King* was a 140-foot-long, 684-ton wooden drill boat, a Canadian scow owned by J.S. Porter and Sons of St. Catherines, Ontario, which was the largest drill boat of the time in Canada. It was engaged in drilling and blasting work to deepen the St. Lawrence Seaway channel. On June 26, it was anchored in the Brockport Narrows, between Brockport, Ontario, and Morristown, New York, on the Canadian side of the river. It was late afternoon, and forty-two members of the crew were still onboard, one shift sleeping in the bunks and the other shift drilling holes into the riverbed in which to place dynamite. The captain, Luther Cushenbeck, happened to be ashore when the unthinkable occurred. Around 4:45 p.m., lightning struck the boat, traveled down the shaft of one of the drills and ignited the dynamite that had just been placed within it. The colossal explosion was instantaneous and catastrophic.

A woman named Mrs. Walklete was watching the vessel from her cottage on the Canadian side and said there was suddenly a great flash, and when the smoke cleared, all she could see were a few survivors thrashing about

The *John B. King*. *From the Archives of the Brockville Museum.*

in the water—nothing more. The daytime foreman on the drill boat, R.A. McNeill of Brockville, was one of the fortunate survivors. He told the *Toronto Globe* on June 27, 1930, that one moment he was standing on deck, and the next instant, he was floating on planking, after the "bottom seemed to go from under the drill boat." It was all so sudden that it was hard to process what had just occurred, but McNeill said that all around him were the bodies of dead men and men still alive and struggling to stay afloat.

The crew of the U.S. Coast Guard cutter *C-G 211* saw the drill boat through the rain and fog about one thousand feet downstream that afternoon and witnessed the bolt of lightning that appeared to plunge straight through the boat. The jolt sent such a violent quiver through their own vessel that they believed their cutter would have foundered had they been any closer than they were at the moment of impact. They saw human bodies tossed two hundred feet in the air, and then the *John B. King* was simply gone. Captain G.B. Lock was in the wheelhouse of the *211* when the *John B. King* was "blown to bits," he told the *Ogdensburg Republican Journal* on June 27, 1930. He described hoisting the danger signal at his vessel's masthead so that other river traffic would divert around the wreckage zone and recalled then

Lightning strike. *NOAA's National Weather Service (NWS) Collection.*

rushing to the scene as it unfolded right before his and his crews' eyes, intent on saving anyone who could still be saved.

The *C-G 211* reached the scene in just four minutes due to its small size and speed. It was storming at the time, with pouring rain, thunder and lightning, and the water had become "wreckage strewn," making the task of finding survivors amid the debris more difficult. The rescue effort was made even more precarious because of the crates of dynamite bobbing in the water around them, and rescuers had no idea if those crates were empty or full. The blast ripped the bottom out of the drill boat, causing it to sink almost immediately. Besides wreckage and bodies, all that remained of the drilling boat was a piece of spar sticking out above the surface. The Coast Guard crew managed to pull nearly a dozen men who had been clinging to scraps of wood out of the water. Some were dazed, some terribly injured and one dead when he hit the water, but the Coast Guardsmen rushed them to the hospital in Brockville. Some of those they picked up, Lock said, never seemed to have touched water at all, since their clothing was dry, yet their injuries indicated they had been thrown into the sky from the explosion and then landed precisely on the wreckage when they fell back down.

After delivering the eleven men to the hospital, the *C-G 211* returned and continued searching well into the night but found no other missing bodies in the vicinity, which led the crew to believe that some were bound to the river bottom by the weight of the hull, rock and stones and others would eventually be found drifting downstream. On June 28, 1930, the *Ogdensburg Republican Journal* stated that one body had been recovered from the wreckage that morning. Two days later, a local diver named George Fisher, who was assisting in treacherous recovery efforts, saw a hand protruding from beneath some timber in the sunken hull. Believing it was a body, Fisher gave it a tug, only to find that there was no body attached to the hand—just a coat sleeve and a hand. He saw no sign of the other thirty missing men believed to have drowned; however, Fisher himself nearly drowned while searching the hull. The *Ogdensburg Republican Journal* of June 30 stated that he became caught in the twisted wreckage and could not break free for more than thirty desperate minutes. Two divers made several unsuccessful attempts to descend and rescue him. Finally, one of them, Ed Boucher, succeeded and "cleared the twisted airline, then collapsed when brought to the surface."

The *Toronto Globe* recalled that another victim of the disaster was a courageous dog named King that the paper had reported on just a few months earlier. King lived on the drill boat and was well loved by all of the men, but he was especially fond of Jack Wylie. In early March, while the drill boat was being repaired, Wylie had been moving machinery across the ice toward the boat when the ice broke beneath him. King heroically jumped into the freezing water and dragged the unconscious Wylie to the surface, saving his life. It was thought (and hoped) that when the *John B. King* exploded that fateful day, Wylie and King crossed the Rainbow Bridge side by side, for he was truly the man's best friend.

On July 10, 1930, the *Ogdensburg Republican Journal* said the body of fifty-four-year-old John Kruzick was discovered floating near Red Mills, New York, in a bay near the shore of farmer Ransom Harper. It had drifted some nineteen miles from the site of the disaster and was found where Leo LaRose's body was retrieved two weeks prior. Harper said he was about to milk his cows when he noticed what looked like a body and took a rowboat out to the spot. Then he felt obliged to do the terrible task of bringing the bloated body to shore and calling the police. While there were no identifying documents on the body, the face appeared disfigured as if from an explosion and a leg had clearly been fractured, leading authorities to believe that the body was one of the *John B. King* crew. It was later positively identified by officials as that of Krazeck. His was the unlucky thirteenth body recovered of the thirty-one who died. Because two bodies from the skiff had been found at that location, stateside, farmers and campers in the Red Mills area were asked to keep a close lookout for more. Sadly, seventeen bodies were never found.

While local divers continued searching for bodies, another drill boat, the *Rockville*, and another crew were dispatched by J.S. Porter and Sons to pick up where the *John B. King* had left off. Whether all the bodies had been recovered or not, dredging the channel in the name of progress would not be stalled by tragic mishap and circumstance. It was all about money, after all. And this time, even more dynamite would be brought in.

On August 11, more than six weeks after the tragedy, Captain T.D. Caldwell, representing the Department of Public Works Canada, told the *Toronto Globe* that recovery efforts were over. The department had spent many dollars and man-hours attempting to locate the remaining victims without success, and it was his belief that it was unlikely the bodies would ever be found, because the wreckage had become an "immovable mass through the terrible force of the explosion." Nothing more could be done. However, the public works did erect a memorial plaque with the names of the victims on the northwest corner of Cockburn Island, well out into the main channel, nearest to where the wreck settled beneath eighty feet of water. The popular dive site is across the river from the Jacques Cartier State Park in Morristown, New York, but it cannot be stressed enough that the site is not for novice divers. As the saying goes, some things are better left untouched. Several divers have actually lost their lives trying to view the wreck.

EIGHT PERSONS PERISH IN CAFÉ EXPLOSION

MASSENA, 1943

Sometimes one disaster begets another. That's how the new year of 1943 began in Massena, New York. On December 30, 1942, one of the worst ice storms in memory struck, knocking out power in the entire town for at least ten days. In some places, it took weeks for the power to be restored. The residents had no choice but to make do with kerosene lamps, candles and fires in their fireplaces. It was back to basics in this hardy community, where citizens are no strangers to improvising. Those of us who recall the 1998 ice storm can relate to the eerie atmosphere of such storms, when the usual sounds and sights are absent. All you can hear are branches snapping in the silence, and all you can see are the faint flickers of candles and lanterns in the darkness. Indeed, the first night of the 1942 storm was said to be Massena's darkest ever. In hindsight, the "darkest night" seemed to portend a much darker night, figuratively speaking, that would unfold several days later, partly because of the ice storm.

On January 4, 1943, Carl King and Ernest Olin, on their way home from work at the Plancor aluminum war plant three miles north of Massena, pulled into the parking lot of Walter H. Hutchins's little store and service station to get some gas for Olin's car. The Plancor plant had recently been completed as part of the wartime expansion program, and employees on their way to or from work often stopped at Hutchins's "lunchroom," as they called it, to fuel up or grab snacks and coffee. The stand was located at the entrance to Hutchins's trailer park in Hutchins Bay on the Old River Road along the bank of the St. Lawrence River, at the end of North Main Street

Hutchins Bay in its heyday. *Courtesy of the Massena Museum (Celine G. Philibert Memorial Culture Centre & Museum).*

(the Pontoon Bridge Road). Because the power was still out, Hutchins's two gas pumps were closed, so Olin and King went inside the unlit store, which was roughly the size of a two-car garage, and Hutchins offered to sell them six gallons of the gas he had siphoned and was keeping in the store. Meanwhile, Maurice Kiah of Ogdensburg pulled his Robillard busload of Plancor plant workers into the dark parking lot so that some of the men could buy some coffee, soda or a snack before their midnight shift. Five men stepped off the bus and into the zero-degree night—they couldn't have imagined that they were marching directly to their doom. Five other plant workers remained on the bus but would bear the burden of what they were about to witness that night for the rest of their lives.

Keeping in mind that everyone's memories of a stressful situation can be slightly different, what happened next has been pieced together to the best of the survivors' and witnesses' recollections. Hutchins, the owner, had already removed three gallons of gas from the larger container and poured it into Olin's car. When Kiah's bus pulled up, Hutchins was refilling the smaller container with three more gallons of gas to complete Olin's order. When the men from the bus came inside, Hutchins set the second can of fuel near the door and asked Olin and King to wait a moment so he could take care of the bus passengers and they could be on their way to work. He had barely made it back around the counter when everything exploded. Somehow, he found his way to a broken window and climbed out. The last thing Hutchins saw was Ernest Sheets coming in the door where Hutchins had just set the gas can. It is believed that somebody lit a match, either to see in the dark or to light their pipe, the gasoline somehow came in contact with the flicker and the sixteen-by-sixteen-foot building exploded, blowing out the entire storefront and scorching eight men beyond recognition in an enormous fireball. Four others were injured, including Hutchins, and they, along with the men on the bus, were all questioned by state troopers trying to determine exactly what happened.

Carl Spearance of Lisbon was burned about the face and hands. He told police he was standing just three feet from the container of gas when it exploded. The blast threw him through the window, which spared his life. Spearance's recollection was that he and eleven others were crowded into the building when the gasoline was being poured into another container. Someone lit a match for light, he said, and that startled the man pouring the gas, who dropped the can on the floor. In the excitement, the man holding the match, Spearance recalled, also became spooked and dropped the match, and that was when the explosion occurred.

Another witness, according to the *Courier and Freeman* of January 6, 1943, was Joe Stacey, who had also stopped by the "shack" on his way to work and witnessed the disaster from the parking lot. Stacey said that Hutchins had just been outside siphoning gas into an open can, and when he stepped back inside carrying the full can, the explosion occurred.

The Massena Volunteer Fire Department rushed to the scene with its pumper, but there was no water supply or hydrants to use at the site, being so far outside the village, so the firefighters returned to the village to gather some five-hundred-gallon drums and the sprinkler tanks. Water was poured on the embers so the remains could be pulled from the rubble and ashes, according to the *Massena Observer* of January 5, 1943, but it froze as soon as it landed. It would be necessary to pour more water on the debris the next morning so firefighters and investigators could continue searching for missing body parts not found in the darkness. The Bureau of Criminal Investigation from Malone and Troop B of the New York State Police arrived to assist, and witnesses and survivors were questioned thoroughly at the Massena substation of the state police headquarters.

Six of the bodies were found lying together at the back of the building, where one of the injured said they must have rushed to, because there was a ticket window used in the summer which they could have climbed out. All eight bodies were removed to the morgue at the Phillips Undertaking Parlor, as it was then called, for identification, which was a grim and time-

Freezing firefighter. *Author's collection.*

consuming task due to the horrific condition of the bodies—some missing arms and legs and most "burned to a crisp," according to the *Ogdensburg Journal* of January 5, 1943—and also due to the fact that the bus driver, who could have identified everyone on his bus, was one of the deceased victims. County coroner Dr. Robert H. Gelder of Winthrop was summoned to begin his inquest. The immediate dead included: Peter J. Black, nineteen, of Ogdensburg; Fred H. LaBounty, nineteen, of Waddington; Carl O. King, twenty-five, of Massena; Glen Cutway, twenty-seven, of Heuvelton; the bus driver, Maurice Kiah, twenty-eight, of Ogdensburg; Ernest F. Olin, thirty-three, of Canton; Louis John Neverette, thirty-six, of Massena; and Barton C. Lawrence, forty-five, of Lisbon.

Ernest Sheets, sixty-three, of Haskell Street in Massena, who was blown into a snowbank by the blast, was taken to the Hepburn Hospital in Ogdensburg for treatment of severe burns on his head, face and arms. He had lost a hand in a dynamite explosion years before the Hutchins explosion, according to the *Advance News* of January 10, 1943. Now this. And to make matters worse, as he lay dying on his hospital bed in an agony beyond description, he was being blamed by some for causing the explosion. An out-of-town newspaper reported that he lit a pipe as he walked into the Hutchins shack and then tossed the match into the container of gas, allegedly believing it was water. Sheets told the reporter of that paper that, true, he did light his pipe, but he had noticed the can of gasoline near the stove when he entered and would never have thrown his match into it. Instead, his usual habit was to break a match in two after blowing it out and crushing it in his hand. He believed the container of gas exploded because it was too close to the stove. According to Sanford Dewey in a story he wrote for *Fire Engineering* magazine on March 1, 1943, Sheets died of his injuries twelve hours after being absolved of blame for the explosion, becoming the ninth victim of the blast—and of the tragic ice storm of 1942–43.

For Walter Hutchins, a hardworking thirty-nine-year-old entrepreneur at the time of the disaster, the story didn't end there. His had already been a life of misfortune, and it would continue to be until the day he died. The *Ogdensburg Journal* of January 19, 1942, said that Hutchins was seriously injured in a head-on collision between the Pontoon Bridge and the Old River Road on January 28, 1942, which resulted in the death of the man driving the other vehicle. Hutchins's jaw was broken in three places, and he suffered a fractured skull that left him semiconscious and hospitalized for a month and a half. On February 9, 1942, just twelve days into his recovery at the Potsdam hospital, a fire of undetermined origin occurred at his home on the Old River Road. While his wife and four young children managed to escape, most of their belongings were lost. That same year, Hutchins, who was simultaneously employed as a tapper at Alcoa, opened the Hutchins Bay trailer park to accommodate aluminum plant employees. The ticket office used in the summer for beachgoers was converted into the lunchroom catering to shift workers in search of soda, coffee, tobacco, candy bars, sandwiches and gasoline. All seemed well for the remainder of the year until the December ice storm knocked power out into January, and then there was the disaster of January 4, 1943, which claimed nine lives on the Hutchins property. And there was more.

The following year, on May 9, 1944, Hutchins's second attempt at opening a restaurant failed when the new Hutchins Restaurant run by his wife was destroyed by fire. Mr. Hutchins was working in Buffalo at the time, and the cause of the fire was undetermined. The building—which had been the former office building of the Bethlehem Steel Corporation on the Hutchinses' property—was destroyed, along with all contents. Never one to give up, Hutchins then opened a dance hall at his "Hutchins Bay Recreation Park," as it had come to be called, in July 1947. An advertisement in the July 10, 1947 *Massena Observer* said there was an orchestra for dancing, a lifeguard on duty at the recreation park and a nearby refreshment stand serving soda, hamburgers and hotdogs.

Five years later, on November 3, 1952, Hutchins who was then forty-eight, was repairing a flat tire on a truck when the jack slipped, and a four-ton water tank rolled off the truck, crushing him to death instantly. It had been a decade of many challenges and perseverance for the well-known family who had contributed so much to the Massena community with their public swimming and recreational facilities, their trailer park, their stores and restaurants and their volunteerism.

LOGAN'S FAULT—5.9 RICHTER SCALE

MASSENA/CORNWALL, 1944

No matter how you slice it, we're on shaky ground here in Northern New York and in St. Lawrence County in particular. According to a *Watertown Daily Times* article dated August 5, 2014, St. Lawrence County had experienced the most recorded earthquakes in the entire state up to that year, coming in at a whopping 153. (By comparison, Jefferson County had a mere 4, and Franklin County came in at 53.) More impressive (or concerning, depending on how you look at it), Massena, New York, holds the title for the largest earthquake in New York State history. It was a magnitude 5.9 on the Richter scale, though some sources place it at 5.8 and some at 6.0. The earthquake that struck at 12:38 a.m. on September 5, 1944, was physically felt as far west as Detroit and as far south as Georgia. The tremor was so powerful that seismographs all the way out in California recorded it. Once the dust settled and calculations and investigations were made, it was determined that the epicenter was at Massena Center, just minutes from our Cornwall, Ontario neighbors with whom we've shared multiple disasters in this book. As such, this disaster has been widely discussed on both sides of the border for generations.

The old-timers agreed that it was the most severe earthquake in many, many years. Although, there had apparently been a real doozy in 1663, when, according to the *Ogdensburg Advance*, a "great roaring sound was heard through the whole extent of Canada." The article of November 30, 1893, went on to say:

The houses seemed to bend first to one side and then to the other. Bells sounded, beams, joists, and planks cracked, and the ground heaved, making the pickets of the palisades dance in a way that would have seemed incredible had we not seen it in diverse places. Everybody was in the streets, animals ran wildly about, children cried, men and women, seized by fright, knew not where to take for refuge; some on their knees in the snow cried for mercy, and others passed the night in prayer. . . . Considerable hills and large tracts of forest slid from their places. Some into the river and some into adjacent valleys.

Lesser earthquakes occurred in January 1832, December 1867, October 1870 and on November 4, 1877. But the earthquake of 1893 aroused anxiety in a whole new generation of people accustomed to blizzards and ice storms and floods, not earth tremors. Luckily, the next "good shake" in these parts didn't happen until September 5, 1944. They blamed it on Logan.

The headlines were telling in the days following the quake. "Hundreds of People, Terrified by Rumbling Noise and Vibrations Rush into Streets in Night Clothes," screamed the *Ogdensburg Journal* of September 5, 1944, adding that the city was "shaken by the most violent earthquake in recorded

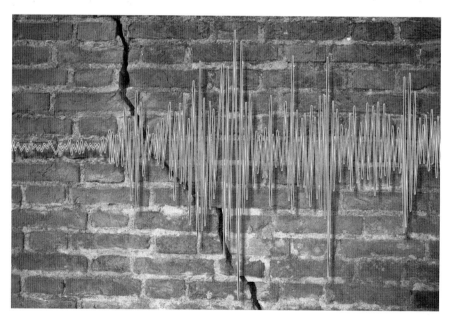

Chimney damage from earthquake. *Author's collection, iStock image.*

history." Hundreds of Ogdensburg residents rushed into the streets in their pajamas, and the phone lines were flooded with calls to the police and to family and neighbors to check on one another's well-being. The *Journal* stated that the quake felt like one's house was being "rocked and pitched." For at least that day, everyone was talking about the earthquake instead of World War II. As bad as they thought it was in their city, the damage there was limited to broken dishes, items falling off shelves, the jarring awake of just about every resident and "a shattered chimney." *A* shattered chimney—just one. In great contrast, Massena and Cornwall experienced damage to a full 90 percent of their chimneys. In fact, so many chimneys were damaged that Massena mayor Rollin Newton requested a list be drawn up of all individuals needing chimney repairs to provide for the deluge of outside contractors eager to take on the work.

"Earthquakes Rock Massena, Chimneys Fall," shouted the *Massena Observer* on E-day. But the first thought of many North Country residents was that their fair town, or the Aluminum Company of America plant in Massena, had become the unlucky target of one of Hitler's new, infamous V-1 robot bombs—not that they were having an earthquake. Although bodily injuries, cuts and scratches from broken glass and falling pictures, were minimal, local physicians made house calls to several homes where people were suffering from "nervous shock," the fashionable term for anxiety and panic disorders at the time. An infant nearly died when it stopped breathing during the earthquake. Dr. F.C. Mason hurried to the residence on Dodge Street and performed artificial respiration on the three-month-old baby, saving its life. George Paquin, seventy-six, of Malone died approximately two hours after the earthquake, and the Franklin County coroner "suggested that it might have resulted from the shock of the earthquake," according to the *Ogdensburg Journal* on September 8, 1944.

Due to damage at every public school in Massena, such as fallen blackboards, cracked plaster, broken glass and damaged chimneys, the superintendent closed all Massena schools until engineers could make their safety inspections. The schools reportedly had 150 windowpanes that were cracked or shattered. The town hall on Main Street was badly damaged, with the front "bulged out" and a large crack between the original building and the addition, so the building—which had shifted from its foundation—was roped off to keep people away until it could be inspected. St. John's Episcopal Church had extensive damage to the marble and brick of its altar, posing a support risk, so the sanctuary was closed for several weeks. At Massena Center (the epicenter of the quake), the old brick church and school building were severely damaged, and decisions had to be made about their fate. Engineers and building inspectors would be kept very busy for quite some time, inspecting public buildings, roads and bridges. North Main and Maple Streets became warped, water mains and plumbing at many residences needed repair and the streetlights went out because the shaking had caused the lighting system to fail.

While the new engine house of the Massena railroad terminal lost quite a lot of plaster, and employees were thrown from their chairs, the passengers on a moving train between Norwood and Massena never felt a thing and wondered why people were standing in the streets when they got off the train. One man who lived near the railroad track in Massena sat up in bed with a start, thinking that a train had jumped the rails and crashed into his house, according to the *Fort Covington Sun* of September 7, 1944. Another individual who lived near the track believed the sound and vibration to be that of a runaway train "speeding by altogether too fast." An exhausted new mother whose husband was overseas was trying to catch a few rare moments of sleep when the earthquake struck. In her disoriented state, she scooped her baby up by its feet and raced outside, where many others were congregating.

Papers from surrounding communities and counties chimed in, giving their yea or nay as to damage in their respective towns. The *Tupper Lake Free Press* of September 7, 1944, announced "Quake Had Tupper Residents 'Quaking'; Did No Damage Here." Potsdam's *Courier & Freeman* of September 6, 1944, ran an article titled, "We Miss Earthquake Damage." From the town of Burke, "no severe damage is reported." And so on and so forth. On the other hand, at daybreak, it became exceedingly clear that extensive damage had been done and precisely where it had been done. While many towns in the North Country felt the convulsions of the quake, the structural damage was concentrated in Massena and Cornwall, primarily. Once that fact was established, the regional papers began offering greater detail about exactly how much damage residents were facing.

The *Courier & Freeman* of September 6, 1944, vividly described destruction to the business sections of Massena and Cornwall, Ontario, where "plate glass windows dropped into the streets." The roof of a Cornwall school caved in. In Massena, it was reported that at least 2,500 chimneys had fallen or been damaged. That's right. It's not a typo. Several *thousand* chimneys in Massena alone were affected by the earthquake—7 out of every 10 chimneys—according to the *Massena Observer* of September 8, 1944. Thank goodness it was not during the winter when their use was a necessity. Hundreds of tombstones were damaged or toppled. Several homes, especially brick houses, were damaged so badly that it was likely they'd have to be torn down and rebuilt. Masons and bricklayers from all around the region were in high demand and had very lucrative work for quite some time. Estimates of property damage to Massena were the greatest this town had ever experienced. And none of it was covered by earthquake insurance. Even today, when we are long overdue for another large quake, how many of us in the Seaway Valley carry earthquake coverage on our homeowner's insurance?

Cornwall, meanwhile, suffered a similar value of property damage and was said to be "in shambles" from collapsed roofs, fallen chimneys, broken windows and cracked walls. The *Fort Covington Sun* of September 7, 1944, told of a Cornwall millworker who was injured when a piece of concrete feel on his head and said "women by the score are reported to have fainted in the streets" in their panic. Schools were extensively damaged and closed until repairs could be made, and absenteeism at local industries was very high for a day or two after the quake.

Ever since Sir William Edmond Logan, founder and first director of the Geological Survey of Canada, discovered the major fault line that is his namesake (Logan's Fault and Logan's Line) in 1860, residents along the St. Lawrence River from Quebec City to Lake Ontario have wondered if the quakes this region sometimes experiences are due to that fault line. Logan's Fault is a primordial zone of thrust faulting in northeastern North America that is well known, especially in the Quebec and St. Lawrence County regions. It parallels the island of Newfoundland, follows the St. Lawrence River Valley and then meanders through the rest of northeastern New York State and down through the Hudson Valley, entering northeastern Pennsylvania before shifting in a southwesterly direction. From around Harrisburg, Pennsylvania, you could take Interstate 81 south all the way down through Virginia and into Tennessee, and you'd be driving on top of Logan's Fault. (Think about that on your next trip south.) Furthermore, the St. Lawrence River, under which much earthquake activity has occurred historically, runs parallel to Canada's 630-mile-long St. Lawrence rift system, which is a well-known seismically active zone. The Ottawa-Bonnechere graben is part of this rift system, and two of the graben's extensions—the Winchester Springs fault and the Gloucester fault—are within the area of the epicenter of the Massena-Cornwall quake of 1944. In addition, Massena is included in the western Quebec earthquake zone. So, there's certainly plenty of faults to go around in this region.

I worked at the St. Lawrence–Franklin D. Roosevelt Power Project on Barnhart Island in Massena for more than three decades. From my window, I could see the bridges from Massena to Cornwall, Ontario, and the Hawkins Point Visitors Center across the river. I could hear the ship's horns as they approached the Eisenhower Lock. The epicenter of the 1944 earthquake was very close to where the power dam, Long Sault Dam, the Massena Intake and the Eisenhower Locks stand, but none of them existed at the time. Construction of these massive projects had not yet begun. But what if this earthquake had occurred during construction or after? And what if an earthquake of that size were to occur today, with all of our dikes and intakes and dams and canals? Surely much thought went into the design of these structures to ensure they could withstand such an earthquake. But they've never been truly tested by Mother Nature in quite the way she tested the ground beneath our feet in 1944. Yes, they are fortresses of steel-reinforced concrete and bricks and mortar, designed to withstand immense amounts of water pushing against their walls. But such materials hardly seem flexible enough to withstand violent shaking and jostling from beneath, which is why concrete, stone and brick structures tend to collapse more than any other types of structures during earthquakes. So, what *if* another strong quake were to strike this region today? What if it was Logan's Fault all over again? Another 5.9 or a 6.0 or more? How would we fare?

FREIGHTER *MILVERTON* COLLISION

WADDINGTON/OGDEN ISLAND, 1947

Another terrible disaster we share with our Canadian neighbors was the devastating collision of the freighter *Milverton* and the loaded oil tanker *Translake* between the village of Iroquois, Ontario, and Waddington, New York, on Wednesday, September 24, 1947. It was a chilly fall morning, when the eastbound Ontario freighter and the westbound Montreal tanker collided nearly head-on at Pine Point near Ogden Island, the narrowest point on the St. Lawrence River at the time with a width of only 1,400 feet.

The freighter exploded and caught on fire immediately, raging wildly (and widely) for days, fueled by the *Milverton*'s 2,500 tons of soft coal and the *Translake*'s massive spill of fuel oil. It was believed that the swift current caused one of the vessels to veer into the course of the other against all attempts to avoid it. Then, either the *Milverton*'s forward fuel oil tanks ignited or a spark from the collision set off thousands of barrels of crude oil that spilled from the tanker into the water and onto the *Milverton* deck. District Attorney Arthur B. Hart of Gouverneur and Coroner Florence Dunlop of Madrid wasted no time in conducting a thorough investigation, along with state police and Coast Guard authorities, even if it was determined that Canadian investigators, who had also launched their own probe of the collision, should take the lead. All information would be shared between American and Canadian officials. Here is what they were able to determine.

The *Milverton* cleared the Cardinal canal (just east of the scene of the disaster) around 5:00 a.m. as the *Translake* tanker, with its Canadian crew of twenty, was making its way west. During interrogation, Captain Chattel,

The *Milverton* on fire. *Copyright Claire Delage, Courtesy of St. Lawrence Piks.*

the pilot and the first mate of the *Translake* all said that no passing signal of any kind was given by the freighter. The general protocol was that ships passing in opposite directions do so portside to portside. However, because of the swift current in that specific channel, the upward bound tanker (the *Translake*) got caught in the current in a starboard to starboard position. Captain Chattel said that when he realized a crash might occur, he put his crew on standby, hoping to somehow beach the tanker to avoid the collision that seemed imminent. Witnesses said the *Milverton* did not have enough warning to avoid collision, and the bow of the *Milverton* caught the *Translake* midship on the starboard side, crushing the *Milverton*'s bow and puncturing the *Translake*'s side, spewing fuel oil in every direction.

A survivor from the *Milverton* told authorities he believed the *Translake* was moving west in an offshore direction from the Canadian side when the two massive vessels struck, puncturing the *Milverton*'s forward fuel tanks and crushing in the foreplates on the starboard side. The deck, he said, became immediately engulfed in flames. There were twenty-three men on board, with several fortunate crew members, including Lookout William Snyder, on leave that day. It was 7:30 a.m.

Clayton Charles Dunnett, the chief engineer of the *Milverton* who was responsible for the engine room every day from 8:00 a.m. to noon and then 8:00 p.m. to midnight, told District Attorney Hart, according to the *Ogdensburg Journal* of September 25, 1947, that he was awakened before his shift by the crash, and his telephone began ringing, but nobody was on the other end. Within seconds, he had thrown on some clothes and was racing for the engine room when the explosion occurred. His way was blocked by flames and smoke and water, so he turned to attempt to go through the dining room and get to the engine room that way, but there, too, he was faced with raging flames. So he slammed the door to the dining room shut and sank to the floor where it was easier to breathe before making another attempt to get through the dining room, where he was then rescued.

A Canadian witness watching from shore told investigators that it looked like the captain was trying desperately to maneuver his burning ship "into a slip at the upper entrance" of Iroquois Canal so his crew stood a better chance of rescue and the fire could be better extinguished. As the *Milverton* swung downstream, shoreline observers could see the wheelsman and captain at their posts, through the smoke and blazing oil, working frantically to minimize loss of life and property.

Mr. and Mrs. Hume Grisdale, whose home was between Iroquois and Morrisburg, Ontario, heard the loud whistles of both boats. The house sat a mere 150 feet from the river, giving them an unobstructed view of the collision. Mrs. Grisdale told the *Ogdensburg Journal* of September 24,

Water on fire with oil spillage. *Author's collection, iStock image.*

1947, that the *Milverton* was moving quickly downstream on the "eight knot current," and the *Translake* was "swinging out into mid-stream after hugging the north shore, as is the custom." She believed that the current must have caught the bow of the tanker, turning it nearly sideways and directly into the path of the freighter, whose bow caved in on impact. The woman said oil from the *Translake* started spurting in all directions, and—just as the survivor mentioned—the entire forward deck of the *Milverton* went up in a mass of flames. The woman immediately called Iroquois for help, which arrived within moments. Residents, first responders and neighbors all got into their boats and rushed into harm's way to save who they could.

Winnipeg fireman Michael Prochnicki was asleep in a cabin with two other *Milverton* employees when they were awakened by the crash. The twenty-year-old stuck his head out the door of the cabin and saw that the entire ship was engulfed in flames, so he and the other young men closed their door and wrapped wet blankets and towels around themselves to try to run through the flames to safety. On deck, he saw his captain, whose face was bloodied and burned, being taken off the burning ship, along with others. And then someone grabbed him and got him off as well. At that early juncture, it was difficult to determine how many men had perished, how many had been rescued and how many were still missing because the wounded were taken to three different hospitals by their various rescuers.

Nobody was injured on Captain Chatel's tanker, which ultimately ran aground near Henderson Bay to await assistance. Meanwhile, the *Milverton*, whose engines were running intermittently, swung first toward the Canadian side but then drifted back out into the current and downstream, still fully engulfed, finally coming to rest on a shoal on the American side between Crapser's Island and the Morrisburg shoreline. The *Transriver* was in the vicinity, so the remaining fuel oil on the *Translake* was transferred to the *Transriver*, allowing the *Translake* to be refloated. The tanker then arrived in Montreal under its own power on Monday, September 29, 1947. The *Cornwall Standard-Freeholder* of October 1, 1947, described the scene as subdued, saying the twenty crew members and officers were "grim-faced" and embarrassed, because they felt condemned by the investigators, media and public for not attempting to help their fellow seamen aboard the *Milverton*. Captain Raoul Chattel of the tanker took offense that he and his crew were being called "almost every name" since the accident and said he would have been risking the lives of his own men to have "sent them into that inferno," and there was nothing they could do but stand by. Yet the shoreline residents, with their little boats and big hearts, raced selflessly into the flames to try to save as many as they could. The true heroes in those early, crucial moments were "scores of Waddington residents and residents of Crapser Island," as well as residents of the Canadian shoreline communities, who went to the rescue without hesitation.

The *Journal* told of five residents from the Iroquois, Ontario area who steered their rowboats through "searing flames" and saved ten men from the burning freighter and two from the water. Edward Casantree, like the Grisdales, heard the ship's whistle and realized it was a distress call. Then he heard a loud explosion from the river and saw the smoke and flames. He and his gathering neighbors could hear heartrending cries for help coming from the ship, so he, Arthur Cornell and his two sons, Gerald and Ronald, and Clare Van Allen all headed out toward the stricken vessel. Casantree said that as they circled the *Milverton*, the captain called down to them and asked if they could take some of the injured to safety in their rowboats. Some of these men had the skin burned entirely off their faces. Casantree took the injured to the American side because it was only 150

Milverton wreckage from the Marcel Quenneville collection. *Courtesy of the Stormont, Dundas and Glengarry Historical Society.*

yards away. While he phoned for help, Van Allen went back out to the burning freighter and brought in three more wounded. Meanwhile, the Cornell brothers picked up two men who had jumped overboard and took them to the Canadian side.

Gerald Cornell said the water was on fire when he and his brother set off toward the ship, but by the time they reached it in about fifteen minutes, the burning water was drifting downstream. He said he and the others got the captain, the pilot, the first mate and the chief engineer off, along with the two who had jumped. The captain told Casantree there were twenty-three aboard the ship but that it was too dangerous for Casantree and the other civilian rescuers to board the ship and search for anyone who might still be there. The risk of further explosions was too high. Initially, six injured were taken to the A. Barton Hepburn Hospital in Ogdensburg, three to the hospital in Massena and two to the hospital in Brockville, Ontario.

The dead included William Robertson, the sixty-year-old second mate from Toronto, who died on the way to the hospital in Ogdensburg. He had just started working for Colonial Steamships Limited, the company that owned the *Milverton*. A day or two before the collision that claimed his life, Frank Gallant, a friend with whom Robertson had lived in Toronto, received a letter from his old pal; its contents remind one of how oblivious we remain (necessarily) of our own impending destinies. It said, in part, according to the *Ogdensburg Journal* of September 26, 1947:

> *Well, I got a job today. I have to go to Thorold tomorrow morning to get on* [the *Milverton*], *as they are unloading there....I just heard this morning that the capt. on the tug that I just got off last week, was washed overboard and drowned last night on Lake Superior. I am glad I got off, or I might have been too.*

William Goldsworthy, third mate on the *Milverton*, died twelve hours after being delivered to the Massena hospital in critical condition. He was just twenty-nine years old and was survived by his parents, four brothers and three sisters, all of whom lived in Newfoundland, except Mrs. Cecil Freeman of Verdun, Quebec. She reached Massena an hour after Goldsworthy died and was tasked with making arrangements to have his body returned to Newfoundland for services and a funeral. She told the press that all the men in her family, including her husband, whom she was trying to reach with the grim news, were seamen.

Official counts of the dead, missing and injured were difficult to ascertain until the *Milverton* cooled off sufficiently for the district attorney, coroner, coroner's physician, undertaker, state police and Canadian officials to board, but the necessary excursion was precarious. Even three days after the collision, another unexplained explosion occurred as the freighter began to settle and buckle with its front end resting on a reef of flat rock ledge, its midship breached and buckling and its unsupported rear settling on the bottom of the river forty feet under. Six bodies, including two in the stern and four in the bow, were recovered from the wreck. On September 26, the body of oiler George McPhail was found below Louisville Landing, where it had drifted some thirteen miles from the wreck. McPhail was identified by a tattoo on his arm. Another man whose body drifted to Massena was identified as Gordon Roberts of Windsor, Ontario. And the body of William Snyder of Morrisburg was recovered on October 3 near the scene of the disaster. By October 4, the death toll had reached twelve. Eleven bodies had been identified; one in the morgue in Cornwall had not. Eight men remained

Milverton recovery operations from the Marcel Quenneville collection. *Courtesy of the Stormont, Dundas and Glengarry Historical Society.*

hospitalized, while two had been released; one man was still unaccounted for. Of the twenty-three men aboard the doomed boat, more than half had died and only one managed to escape without injury. *One.*

Canadian government marine officials asked the Sarnia and Colonial Steamships Company to remove the wreck from its resting place off Ogden Island. It would not be an easy task in the swift current, and it was nothing that salvage crews were eager to endeavor. Plus, with winter just around the corner, removal would likely not take place before spring, anyway. Luckily, the wreckage was not in the shipping lane. The following year, from August to November 1948, Port Colborne Iron Works was awarded the job of salvaging the wreck, and it did so successfully (with ten men working ten-hour days, seven days a week until the job was complete). Once raised, the *Milverton* was towed to the Bruce Cole Company dock in Morrisburg by two powerful tugboats, where it was anchored for the winter.

In late March 1949, the *Milverton* was towed under its own power to Port Weller, Ontario, in St. Catherines to be refitted and renamed. It emerged in July as the *Clary Foran*. On September 10, 1949, the vessel passed the infamous site of its almost watery grave near Ogden Island. It passed respectfully through the waters of its prior existence, where so many good seamen it once carried had gone down violently with it. *Clary Foran* passed the region where it, as the *Milverton*, had been the object of one of the worst maritime disasters the mighty St. Lawrence River had ever seen just two Septembers before.

BIBLIOGRAPHY

Note: The newspaper articles listed below can be viewed online at the NYS Historic Newspapers website: http://nyshistoricnewspapers.org.

Chapter 1. EF5 Tornado

Advance News. "4 Tornadoes Have Struck North Section." July 26, 1935.

Essex County Republican. "Tornado and Hail Storm." September 27, 1845.

Herald-Recorder. "Tornado Kills Wife of Farmer." July 26, 1935.

New York Times. "A Terrible Tornado—Village of Chateaugay in Ruins—Over One Hundred Buildings Destroyed." July 9, 1856.

Ogdensburg Advance. "One Killed, 3 Injured as Cyclone Passes Through Philadelphia." July 21, 1935.

Ogdensburg Journal. "Girl Second Victim of Wind Storm." July 22, 1935.

Watertown Jeffersonian. "Awful Tornado." September 30, 1845.

Wikipedia. "Enhanced Fujita Scale." https://en.wikipedia.org/wiki/Enhanced_Fujita_scale.

Chapter 2. Watertown in Ruins

Aurora Regional Fire Museum. "Timeline of Fires and Firefighting Events." www.auroraregionalfiremuseum.org.

Franklin Gazette. "Watertown Nearly Destroyed by Fire." May 24, 1849.

GenDisasters. "Watertown, NY Fire, May 1849." www.gendisasters.com.

New-York Semi-Weekly Tribune. "Disastrous Fire at Watertown." May 19, 1849.

St. Lawrence Republican. "Great Conflagration. Watertown in Ruins." May 15, 1849.

Watertown Daily Times. "200th Anniversary of Watertown Fire Department Exhibit Opens Monday at Historical Society." September 10, 2017.

Watertown Jeffersonian Extra. "The Great Fire at Watertown—List of Losses and Insurance." May 23, 1849.

Chapter 3. Whitney Marble Company Boiler Explosion

Courier & Freeman. "Fearful Boiler Explodes at Gouverneur." May 7, 1884.

Daily Journal. "Fearful Boiler Explosion at Gouverneur." May 5, 1884.

Economic History Association. "History of Workplace Safety in the United States, 1880–1970." http://eh.net.

Gouverneur Free Press. "A Boiler Explodes." May 7, 1884.

———. "Boiler Explosion." May 14, 1884.

New York Times. "Terrific Boiler Explosion." May 4, 1884.

Watertown Daily Times. "Expert Testimony." May 8, 1884.

Chapter 4. Carthage in Ruins

Carthage-Wilna Fire District. "The Great Carthage Fire." carthagenyfire.com.

Daily Journal. "Great Fire at Carthage." October 21, 1884.

Lewis County Democrat. "The Great Carthage Fire." October 22, 1884.

North Country at Work. "Sketch of 1884 Fire in West Carthage and Carthage." www.northcountryatwork.org.

North Country Public Radio. "The Great Fire of 1884." hwww.northcountrypublicradio.org.

Watertown Re-Union. "Carthage in Ruins." October 22, 1884.

Watertown Times. "The Carthage Relief." October 25, 1884.

———. "For Relief." October 24, 1884.

———. "The Movement in New York." October 25, 1884.

———. Notes. October 25, 1884.

Chapter 5. Blown to Atoms

New York Times. "A Dynamite Explosion." February 25, 1886.

———. "A Terrific Explosion. Nitro-Glycerine Quickly Demolishes a Powder Factory." January 12, 1887.

Plattsburgh Republican. "Crab Island Too Near." February 12, 1887.

———. "Nitro Glycerine Explosion." February 27, 1886.

———. "Plattsburgh's Earthquake." January 15, 1887.

Plattsburgh Sentinel. "Blown to Atoms." January 14, 1887.

———. "Dynamite Explosion at Plattsburgh." February 26, 1886.

———. Notes. February 11, 1887.

Chapter 6. Barnum & Bailey Circus Train Wreck

Advance News & St. Lawrence Weekly Democrat. "Barnum and Bailey's Train Wrecked." August 19, 1889.

Commercial Advertiser. "Barnum's Show Wrecked." August 28, 1889.

Free Press. "The Wreck." August 30, 1889.

Ithaca Daily Journal. "Circus Train Wrecked." August 23, 1889.

Norwood News. "One of Barnum & Bailey's Trains Wrecked." August 27, 1889.

Watertown Re-Union. "The Circus." August 21, 1889.

Watertown Times. "Barnum & Bailey's Wreck." August 24, 1889.

Chapter 7. The Great Floods

Gouverneur Journal. "The Oswegatchie Booms." September 10, 1890.

Journal and Republican. "Worse Than Fire." September 18, 1890.

Ogdensburg Journal. Notes (re. flood). September 18, 1890.

———. "The Raging Waters." September 15, 1890.

———. "Wrecked by Floods." September 17, 1890.

On the St. Lawrence and *Clayton Independent*. "Heavy Damages by the Floods." September 19, 1890.

Pulaski Democrat. "The Great Rain Fall of 1890." September 18, 1890.

St. Lawrence Herald. Notes (re. flood). September 19, 1890.

Watertown Herald. "Rain and Flood." September 13, 1890.

———. "Water's Work." September 20, 1890.

Watertown Re-Union. "Big Floods." September 17, 1890.

Watertown Times. "The Story of the Big Flood." September 15, 1890.

Chapter 8. *The* Hartford *Goes Down—All Hands Lost*

Ogdensburg Advance and *St. Lawrence Weekly Democrat*. "Lost with All on Board." October 18, 1894.
Ogdensburg Daily Journal. "Furious Storm." October 12, 1894.
———. "Lost with All on Board." October 12, 1894.
———. "The Wreck of the Hartford—The Skipper's Little Daughter Was but One Year Old." October 15, 1894.
On the St. Lawrence and *Clayton Independent*. "Hartford Lost." October 19, 1894.
———. "The Hartford Wreck Visited." November 2, 1894.
Oswego Daily Palladium. "Echoes from the Wreck." October 15, 1894.
Sandy Creek News. "Coroner's Inquest." October 25, 1894.
Shampine, Dave. "A Long-Ago Lake Ontario Tragedy." *Watertown Daily Times*, November 22, 2009.
Watertown Re-Union. "Terrible Disaster." October 17, 1894.

Chapter 9. *Appalling Bridge Collapse*

Catskill Archive. "The Fall of a Bridge at Cornwall, Ontario." www.catskillarchive.com.
Chateaugay Journal. "Fell to Death." September 8, 1898.
———. Notes. September 15, 1898.
Commercial Advertiser. "Awful Calamity." September 14, 1898.
Gazette. "Fearful Disaster Near Hogansburg." September 9, 1898.
Malone Palladium. "The Cornwall Disaster." September 15, 1898.
Massena Observer. "Appalling Disaster." September 8, 1898.
———. "Foundation Faulty." November 9, 1898.
———. Notes. September 15, 1898.
———. "A $20,000 Damage Suit." March 30, 1899.
Ogdensburg Journal. "Cornwall Bridge Disaster." September 15, 1898.
———. "Funeral of Frank LaVigne, a Victim of the Cornwall Bridge Disaster." September 12, 1898.
———. "No Bodies Recovered Yet." September 10, 1898.
———. Notes (re. Henry Davis). September 23, 1898.
Sentinel. "Bridge Fell Sixty Feet." September 8, 1898.

St. Lawrence Herald. Notes (re. three bodies). September 30, 1898.

Chapter 10. Tupper Lake in Ruins

Adirondack News. "The Tupper Lake Fire." August 5, 1899.
Elizabethtown Post. "Wiped Out by Fire." August 3, 1899.
Herkimer Democrat. "Fire at Tupper Lake." August 2, 1899.
Malone Palladium. "Fire Swept! Tupper Lake in Ruins!" August 3, 1899.
Massena Observer. "Tupper Lake Fire Swept." August 3, 1899.
New York Times. "A New York Town Destroyed." July 31, 1899.
Norwood News. "$175,000 Fire at Tupper Lake." August 1, 1899.
Ogdensburg Journal. "Whole Village Destroyed." August 2, 1899.

Chapter 11. Snowbound

Chateaugay Record and *Franklin County Democrat.* "Funeral of Victims of Storm Held Saturday." February 3, 1928.
———. "Two Young Girls Meet Death in Winter's Worst Storm on Way Home from School." January 27, 1928.
Malone Farmer. "Two Children Frozen to Death in Blizzard That Raged Wednesday." February 1, 1928.
———. "Wednesday's Storm Caused the Death of Third Victim." February 1, 1928.
Norwood News. "The Worst Storm of the Season." March 6, 1900.
Ogdensburg Advance and St. Lawrence Weekly Democrat. Notes (re. blizzard). February 29, 1912.
Ogdensburg Journal. "Great Blizzard of 1900." March 2, 1900.
———. Notes (re. blizzard). February 24, 1912.
———. "Story of Blizzard." March 2, 1900.
Potsdam Herald-Recorder. Notes (re. blizzard). March 1, 1912.
Republican-Journal. "Dying Children Bade Mother Good-Bye as Death Neared." January 28, 1928.

Chapter 12. Adirondack Inferno

Chateaugay Journal. "Adirondack Forest Fires." May 7, 1903.
Commercial Advertiser. "The Forest Fires." June 10, 1903.
Courier & Freeman. "Fierce Forest Fires." May 6, 1903.
Hicks, Harry W. "Inferno in the Adirondacks." *North Country Life* (Fall 1948).
Malone Farmer. "Fierce Forest Fires." May 6, 1903.
———. "Forest Fires." June 10, 1903.
———. "More About Forest Fires." May 13, 1903.
———. Notes. May 13, 1903.
———. Notes. July 8, 1903.
Massena Observer. "Forest Fires Burn a Million Acres." June 4, 1903.
———. "Great Damage by Forest Fires." June 11, 1903.
Medina Daily Journal. "Forest Fires Raging." May 1, 1903.
Northern Tribune. "Awful Forest Fires." May 1, 1903.
———. "Boy and Horse Burned." May 8, 1903.
Norwood News. "Franklin County News." June 16, 1903.
———. "Great Forest Fires." May 5, 1903.
———. Notes. May 12, 1903.
———. Notes. June 9, 1903.
———. Noted. June 19, 1903.
Ogdensburg Advance and *St. Lawrence Weekly Democrat*. "Forest Fires Raging." May 7, 1903.
Plattsburgh Daily Press. "Fierce Forest Fires." May 1, 1903.
———. "Fishermen Hemmed In." May 4, 1903.
Plattsburgh Republican. "More Adirondack Forest Fires." May 16, 1903.
Plattsburgh Sentinel and *Clinton County Farmer*. "Adirondack Fires." June 5, 1903.
———. "Beauty Spots Uninjured." June 19, 1903.
———. "Forest Fires Still Raging." May 29, 1903.
Pokeepsie Evening Enterprise. Notes (from Plattsburgh). May 1, 1903.
St. Lawrence Herald. "Adirondack Fires." May 15, 1903.
———. "More Fires in Adirondacks." May 15, 1903.
———. Notes (re. Adirondack Lodge). June 19, 1903.
Ticonderoga Sentinel. "Forest Fires." June 11, 1903.

Chapter 13. Runaway Trains

Elizabethtown Post. "Mineville." February 23, 1905.

New York Times. "Train Plunges Through Draw." August 2, 1903.

Plattsburgh Daily Press. "Splinter Through Head." August 3, 1903.

Plattsburgh Republican. "Fatal Railroad Wreck at Cooperville." August 8, 1903.

Plattsburgh Sentinel and *Clinton County Farmer*. "Train in Chazy River." August 7, 1903.

Ticonderoga Sentinel. "Locomotive Ran Away." February 16, 1905.

———. Notes (re. Brakeman Frazer). August 6, 1903.

———. "An Ore Train Runs Away Over Mountain." February 23, 1905.

Chapter 14. North Lawrence in Ruins

Chateaugay Record and *Franklin County Democrat*. "North Lawrence Fire Swept." July 12, 1907.

Facts and Fallacies. "No. Lawrence Fire Swept." July 11, 1907.

Fitchburg Sentinel. "Village Destroyed by Fire." July 5, 1907.

Herald Advertiser. "Disastrous Fire at No. Lawrence." July 9, 1907.

Madrid Herald. "North Lawrence Fire." July 11, 1907.

Malone Farmer. "Disastrous Fire." July 10, 1907.

Massena Observer. "North Lawrence Nearly Wiped Out." July 11, 1907.

Norwood News. "Aid Will Be Received." July 16, 1907.

———. "The North Lawrence Fire Losses." July 16, 1907.

Plattsburgh Republican. "Disastrous Fire at North Lawrence." July 13, 1907.

Plattsburgh Sentinel. "Appeal for the North Lawrence Fire Sufferers." July 12, 1907.

Stewart, Bob. "Wag of the Tail: Reflecting on Pet Ownership." In *Enriching Our Lives with Animals*, edited by John Jaimeson, Tony Bannerman and Selena Wong, 97–105. Toronto, ON: Petlove Press, 2007.

"Typical Fires and Their Lessons. Conflagration at North Lawrence, N.Y." *Insurance Engineering* 14, no. 171 (1907).

Chapter 15. Frightful Calamity at Benson Mines

Daily Journal. "Frightful Calamity at Benson Mines." August 17, 1908.

———. "Mine Victims Buried." August 18, 1908.

Journal and Republican. "Five Miners Were Killed." August 20, 1908.

Norwood News. "Benson Mines Disaster." August 18, 1908.

Watertown Herald. "Four Miners Killed." August 22, 1908.

Watertown Re-Union. "Five Men Killed." August 19, 1908.

Chapter 16. Seven Meet Death in River

Commercial Advertiser. Notes (re. Captain Weston C. Cline). May 21, 1912.
———. "Seven Meet Death in River." August 8, 1911.
Malone Farmer. "Seven Drowned at Massena." August 2, 1911.
Massena Observer. "Steamer Sirius (ad)." August 3, 1911.
———. "Steamer Turns Turtle—Seven Are Drowned." August 3, 1911.
———. "Today Is 30th Anniversary of Grasse River Tragedy, Steamer Sank, 7 Drowned." August 1, 1941.
Norwood News. Notes (re. Steamer Venus). May 21, 1912.
———. "Seven Drowned Near Massena." August 8, 1911.
Ogdensburg Advance and *St. Lawrence Weekly Democrat.* "Coroner Investigating." August 10, 1911.
———. "Ferry Steamer Swamped." August 3, 1911.
Ogdensburg Journal. "Capt. Cline Is Raising the Sirius." August 10, 1911.
———. "Double Funeral Tomorrow for the Misses Parker." August 2, 1911.
———. "Medal for 'Sirius' Hero?" February 15, 1913.
Sun. "Another Calamity." August 1, 1911.
Watertown Re-Union. Notes (re. Sirius). August 5, 1911.

Chapter 17. Thousand Island Park in Ruins

Cape Vincent Eagle. "Thousand Island Park in Ruins." July 11, 1912.
Commercial Advertiser. "Hotels and Cottages Destroyed." July 16, 1912.
Journal and Republican. "Fire at Thousand Island Park." July 11, 1912.
Middleton Daily Times-Press. "Thousand Island Park Fire Swept." July 10, 1912.
Ogdensburg Journal. "Thousand Island Park Devastated by Fire." July 9, 1912.

Chapter 18. Hotel Fire Claims Seven Lives

Chateaugay Record. "Awful Holocaust." April 18, 1913.
Commercial Advertiser. "Seven Dead in Malone Fire." April 22, 1913.
Essex County Republican. "Seven Burned to Death in Malone Hotel Blaze." April 25, 1913.
Journal and Republican and Lowville Times. "Seven Persons Perish in Fire at Malone." April 24, 1913.
Malone Farmer. "An Awful Tragedy." April 23, 1913.

New York Times. "Hotel Fire Costs 7 Lives." April 18, 1913.

Plattsburgh Sentinel. "Acquitted of Manslaughter." April 4, 1916.

Stevens Point Daily Journal. "Nine Die in Hotel Blaze." April 18, 1913.

Sun. "Hotel Fire Costs 7 Lives." April 24, 1913.

Syracuse Herald. "Nine Dead, One Missing, Many Injured in Malone Hotel Fire." April 17, 1913.

Tupper Lake Herald. "Community Greatly Shocked by Tragic Death of Philip O'Connor in Malone Hotel Fire." April 25, 1913.

Chapter 19. Bradley Powder House Explosion

Commercial Advertiser. "Watertown Boys Used Powder House for Target." May 11, 1915.

Ogdensburg Advance and *St. Lawrence Weekly Democrat.* "Watertown Shaken by Dynamite." May 13, 1915.

Ogdensburg Journal. "Coroner Will Probe Blowup in Watertown." May 10, 1915.

Watertown Herald. "Funerals of Explosion Victims." May 15, 1915.

———. "Investigating Explosion." May 15, 1915.

Watertown Re-Union. "Explosion Was Felt at Gouverneur." May 12, 1915.

———. "15,000 Visit Scene of the Accident." May 12, 1915.

———. "Two Killed by Explosion." May 12, 1915.

Chapter 20. Deadly Christmas Eve Munitions Plant Explosion

Courier & Freeman. "Former Baptist Pastor." January 1, 1919.

———. "Seven Dead in Explosion." January 1, 1919.

Journal and Republican. "Six Killed by Explosion." December 26, 1918.

Ogdensburg Republican-Journal. "Six Killed and Nineteen Injured in Explosion in Watertown Munition Plant." December 26, 1918.

Plattsburgh Sentinel. "Six Killed at Watertown." December 27, 1918.

Shampine, Dave. "A Deadly Blast, Seven Killed in Christmas Eve 1918 World War I J.B. Wise Plant Explosion." *Watertown Daily Times*, March 11, 2001.

Syracuse Journal. Note (re. compensation). March 11, 1919.

Watertown Daily Times. "Explosion 50 Years Ago Recalled." December 24, 1968.

———. "Gets $23.46 a Week for Death of Sons." March 5, 1919.

———. "J.B. Wise Explosion Two Years Ago." December 24, 1920.

———. "Worst Explosion in City's History." July 13, 1922.

Chapter 21. Exploding Shell Kills Eight Children

Cape Vincent Eagle. "District Attorney Criticizes Buffalo Artillerymen in Report on Shell Horror." August 31, 1922.
Ogdensburg Republican-Journal. "Eight Children Die in Shell Explosion." July 17, 1922.
————. "Exploding Shell Kills 8 Children." July 17, 1922.
————. "Shell Found at Pine Plains 2 Years Ago." July 14, 1922.
Sandy Creek News. "Dud Shell Explodes." July 13, 1922.

Chapter 22. Au Sable Forks Is Prey to Flames

Adirondack Record-Elizabethtown Post. "Au Sable Forks Is Prey to Flames!" May 14, 1925.
Plattsburgh Sentinel. "AuSable Asks Assistance in Its Extremity." May 19, 1925.
————. "$50,000 Asked for Sufferers." May 19, 1925.
————. "Plattsburgh's Hero Fireman Loses Fight." May 19, 1925.
————. "Plattsburgh Theatre Will Give Benefit." May 19, 1925.
Post-Star. "Stores, Churches, and Homes Destroyed by AuSable Fire." May 15, 1925.

Chapter 23. Tenement Fire Claims Seven Lives

Adirondack Record-Elizabethtown Post. "Saranac Lake Fire Takes Seven Lives." July 9, 1925.
Chateaugay Record. "Saranac Lake Tragedy, Seven Burned to Death." July 10, 1925.
Dallas Morning News. "Seven Persons Dead in Blaze." July 5, 1925
Davenport Democrat and Leader. "Seven People Burn to Death." July 5, 1925.
Essex County Republican. "Saranac Lake Fire Sufferer Returns Home." August 21, 1925.
Lake Placid News. "Investigation Follows Saranac Lake Fire." July 17, 1925.
Norwood News. "Meet Death in Saranac Lake Fire." July 8, 1925.
Ogdensburg Republican-Journal. "Start of Probe of Fire at Saranac Lake That Took Lives of Seven." July 6, 1925.
Plattsburgh Sentinel. "Investigation Conducted in Saranac Fire." July 7, 1925.
————. "Saranac Inquest Adjourned Again." July 10, 1925.

———. "Start of Probe of Fire at Saranac Lake That Took Lives of Seven." January 12, 1926.

Record-Post. "Mrs. Geo. Dukett Slowly Recovering." November 19, 1925.

Ticonderoga Sentinel. "Seven Die in Saranac Lake Fire." July 9, 1925.

Chapter 24. Thirty Die in Sinking of the John B. King

Lunman, Kim. "Film Pays Tribute to the Wreck of the J.B. King," Thousand Islands Life. https://thousandislandslife.com.

Maritime History of the Great Lakes. "John B. King, Exploded, 26 May 1930." http://images.maritimehistoryofthegreatlakes.ca/58864/data.

Ogdensburg Republican-Journal. "Believe More Bodies May Be Near the City." July 11, 1930.

———. "Body of Man Killed in Drill Boat Blast Is Found East of City." July 10, 1930.

———. "Captain of Cutter Tells About Rescue." June 27, 1930.

———. "Diver Nearly Loses Life in Rescue Work." June 30, 1930.

———. "Divers Find One Body in Boat Debris." June 28, 1930.

———. "Dynamiting Work to Be Carried On." July 2, 1930.

———. "Local Diver Recovers Hand from Wreckage." June 30, 1930.

———. "Only 2 Severe Storms During Month of June." July 2, 1930.

Plattsburgh Sentinel. "Lightning Strikes Dynamite—21 Dead." June 27, 1930.

Wikipedia. "John B. King Explosion." https://en.wikipedia.org/wiki/John_B._King_explosion.

Chapter 25. Eight Persons Perish in Café Explosion

Adirondack Daily Enterprise. "Man Crushed to Death." November 4, 1952.

Advance News. "Denies He Caused the Gas Blast." January 10, 1943.

Courier and Freeman. "8 Die in Explosion and Fire at Massena Service Station." January 6, 1943.

Dewey, Sanford D. "Gasoline Explosion Kills Eight." *Fire Engineering Magazine*, March 1, 1943.

Fitchburg Sentinel. "Eight Persons Perish in Blast at Massena, N.Y." January 5, 1943.

Massena Observer. "8 Men Burn to Death." January 5, 1943.

———. "Funerals Held for Fire Victims." January 8, 1943.

———. "Hutchins Restaurant Destroyed." May 9, 1944.

———. "Inquest Date into Tragedy Not Yet Set." January 8, 1943.

———. "New Dance Hall (ad)." July 10, 1947.

———. Notes (re. Hutchins Bay). June 25, 1959.

———. Notes (re. Walter Hutchins). February 3, 1942.

———. Notes (re. Walter Hutchins), February 24, 1942.

———. Notes (re. Walter Hutchins). February 11, 1952.

———. "Services for Mr. Hutchins Held Today." November 6, 1952.

———. "$75 Million for State Parks." October 25, 1960.

———. "Tuesday 16th Anniversary of Area's Worst Ice Storm." January 1, 1959.

Ogdensburg Journal. "8 Persons Perish in Cafe Explosion Near Massena; Two Are Ogdensburg Men." January 5, 1943.

———. "Family at Massena Lose Home." February 10, 1942.

———. "Man Killed in Head on Car Accident." January 29, 1942.

———. "Probe of Massena Explosion and Fire That Took 8 Lives Shows Gas Stood in Water Pail." January 8, 1943.

———. "Victim Massena Tragedy Patient in Hepburn Hospital Denies That He Threw Match That Caused Blast." January 6, 1943.

Syracuse Herald-Journal. "Stock Is Saved as Barn Burns." May 4, 1953.

Chapter 26. Logan's Fault—5.9 Richter Scale

Advance News. "Logan's Fault." September 10, 1944.

———. Notes (re. earthquake). September 10, 1944.

———. "Ogdensburg Felt Earth Shock Last Night." September 10, 1944.

Alcock, F.J. "Logan's Fault." *Journal of the Royal Astronomical Society of Canada* 39 (August 1945): 213.

Chateaugay Record. "Chateaugay Residents Shocked by Severe Earthquake." September 8, 1944.

———. Notes (re. earthquake). September 8, 1944.

Commercial Advertiser. "Earthquake Shock Is Distinctly Felt." September 5, 1944.

Courier Freeman. "Quake Shakes Northern New York Monday Nite." September 6, 1944.

———. "We Miss Earthquake Damage." September 6, 1944.

"Documents of the SENATE of the State of New York. One Hundred and Thirty-Fourth Session." Albany, NY: J.B. Lyon Company, State Printers, 1911.

Fort Covington Sun. "Earthquake Early Tuesday Morning Was Worst Ever; Massena, Cornwall Suffer." September 7, 1944.

Hammond Advertiser. "North Alarmed by Quake Tuesday A.M." September 7, 1944.

Massena Observer. "Call Chamber Office If You Need Chimney Repaired." September 15, 1944.

———. "Cornwall Newspaper Tells of Quake Damage There." September 8, 1944.

———. "Earthquakes Rock Massena, Chimneys Fall." September 5, 1944.

———. "Massena Starts Repairing Damage Caused by Record-Breaking Quake." September 8, 1944.

———. "Meeting Called to Decide Future of Brick Church." September 15, 1944.

———. "Next Tremors Expected to Be Light, Eminent Seismologist Studies Effects." September 12, 1944.

———. "Town Board to Study Roof Plans." September 19, 1944.

Ogdensburg Advance. "Earthquake Shocks." November 30, 1893.

Ogdensburg Journal. "Another Earth Tremor Felt Here Saturday Evening, Canton Center of Disturbance, Near Panic in Massena." September 11, 1944.

———. "Damage to Massena from Earthquake Mounts to $750,000 to $1,000,000, Nearly Every Building Suffered." September 6, 1944.

———. "The Earthquake Last Night." September 5, 1944.

———. "Hundreds of People, Terrified by Rumbling Noise and Vibrations Rush into Streets in Night Clothes." September 5, 1944.

———. "Quake May Have Killed Brother of Local Woman." September 8, 1944.

———. "2,500 Massena Chimneys Damaged by Quake, Contractors Rush Bricklayers to Village, Four New Shocks Felt." September 8, 1944.

———. "Water Lines, Windows Broken in Massena, Chimneys Toppled as Damage Mounts to Thousands." September 5, 1944.

Revetta, Frank A. "The Massena-Cornwall Earthquake of September 5, 1944." (St. Lawrence County Historical Association) *Quarterly*, October 1984.

Revetta, Frank A., and Adam Spinner. "Are Earthquakes in the Massena, New York Area Related to the Gloucester and Winchester Springs Faults?" Presentation at Northeastern Section of the Geological Society of America, 40th Annual Meeting, March 14–16, 2005.

Tupper Lake Free Press and *Tupper Lake Herald.* "Quake Had Tupper Residents 'Quaking'; Did No Damage Here." September 7, 1944.

Watertown Daily Times. "Earthquakes, We're in the Zone." August 5, 2014.

Chapter 27. Freighter Milverton *Collision*

Advance News. "Capt. Pain Still in Hepburn Hospital." October 12, 1947.

Commercial Advertiser. "Collier Milverton Written Off by Owners as Total Loss." October 7, 1947.

————. "Freighter-Tanker Collide Near Waddington With Loss of Life." September 30, 1947.

Massena Observer. "Milverton Makes Her First Trip." September 15, 1949.

————. "2 Men Recovering from Burns at Massena Hospital." October 2, 1947.

————. "2 or 3 Men Still Missing, Positive Identification Made of Body Found Sunday." October 2, 1947.

————. "Workmen Expect Milverton to Be Re-Floated by Nov. 1, Salvage Work Now Being Rushed." October 4, 1948.

Ogdensburg Journal. "Body of Milverton Crew Man Found in St. Lawrence Identified; Loss of Ship Set at $300,000 by Owners." October 1, 1947.

————. "Canadian Government Asks Removal of Milverton Wreck, Ship Abandoned as Total Loss." October 3, 1947.

————. "Mate Who Died Felt Lucky in His New Post." September 26, 1947.

————. "Milverton Starts to Settle Following Another Explosion; Six Bodies Taken from Ship." September 27, 1947.

————. "Milverton To Be Refitted." April 6, 1949.

————. "Morrisburg Sailor's Body Found at Head of Island at Waddington; Was Aboard Ill-Fated Milverton." October 4, 1947.

————. "Rivermen Played Heroic Part in Rescuing Survivors of Collier Milverton's Crew." September 26, 1947.

————. "Searchers Board Burning Collier to Hunt for Nine Missing Sailors." September 25, 1947.

————. "Six Bodies Taken from Burned Ship in Channel Near Waddington Today; Toll Stands at 8 Dead; 3 Missing." September 26, 1947.

————. "SS *Milverton* to Be Rebuilt." March 31, 1949.

————. "2 Dead, 11 Missing in River Collision." September 24, 1947.

ABOUT THE AUTHOR

Cheri Farnsworth has written the following regional titles (some sunder the name of Cheri Revai): *Haunted Northern New York* (Volumes 1–4, 2002–10), *Haunted Massachusetts* (2005), *Haunted New York* (2005), *Haunted Connecticut* (2006), *Haunted New York City* (2008), *The Big Book of New York Ghost Stories* (2009), *Haunted Hudson Valley* (2010), *Adirondack Enigma: The Depraved Intellect and Mysterious Life of North Country Wife Killer Henry Debosnys* (2010), *Murder & Mayhem in Jefferson County* (2010), *Murder & Mayhem in St. Lawrence County* (2010), *Alphabet Killer: The True Story of Rochester's 'Double Initial'* *Murders* (2010) and *Wicked Northern New York* (2011).

She enjoys researching regional history, especially crime and disaster, and finds the connection between history and the paranormal intriguing as well. Farnsworth is retired and lives in Massena, New York, with her husband, three peculiar cats and one crazy, cuddly Labradoodle.

Visit us at
www.historypress.com